**Managing Change
Step by Step**

South Sefton
6th Form College

Books that make you better

Books that make you better. That make you *be* better, *do* better, *feel* better. Whether you want to upgrade your personal skills or change your job, whether you want to improve your managerial style, become a more powerful communicator, or be stimulated and inspired as you work.

Prentice Hall Business is leading the field with a new breed of skills, careers and development books. Books that are a cut above the mainstream – in topic, content and delivery – with an edge and verve that will make you better, with less effort.

Books that are as sharp and smart as you are.

Prentice Hall Business.
We work harder – so you don't have to.

For more details on products, and to contact us, visit
www.pearsoned.co.uk

Managing Change
Step by Step

All you need to build a plan and make it happen

Richard Newton

PEARSON
Prentice Hall
BUSINESS

Harlow, England • London • New York • Boston • San Francisco • Toronto • Sydney • Singapore • Hong Kong
Tokyo • Seoul • Taipei • New Delhi • Cape Town • Madrid • Mexico City • Amsterdam • Munich • Paris • Milan

PEARSON EDUCATION LIMITED

Edinburgh Gate
Harlow CM20 2JE
Tel: +44 (0)1279 623623
Fax: +44 (0)1279 431059
Website: www.pearsoned.co.uk

First published in Great Britain in 2007

ISBN: 978-0-273-71177-3

British Library Cataloguing-in-Publication Data
A catalogue record for this book is available from the British Library

10 9 8 7 6 5 4 3 2 1
11 10 09 08 07

Typeset in 11/14pt Minion by 30
Printed and bound in by Ashford Colour Press Ltd., Gosport

The Publisher's policy is to use paper manufactured from sustainable forests.

This book is dedicated to Amelia and Edward Brooks

Contents

Introduction

I want to start with some good news. Although managing change can be complex and intense, if you approach it in a structured way, with realistic expectations, it should never be daunting. Managing change successfully will draw on a wide range of skills, but it is not incomprehensible black magic! With a little work it is straightforward to understand. This book is here to help you with clear, uncomplicated, practical advice that you can apply immediately.

The structured approach to managing change has become widely known, obviously enough, as change management. But why bother with change management? Firstly, good change management increases the effectiveness of your change initiatives whether they are chosen by you or thrust upon you. Secondly, effective change management significantly reduces the risk of major problems when implementing change, whether you are totally in control of change or frantically responding to it. Finally, efficient change management will make your own life easier when you are involved in any change situation, and you will become more valuable to your employer.

Overused mantras such as 'the pace of change is ever increasing', and 'there is no constant but change', are rolled out continuously at management presentations. Underneath these overworn, usually unquestioned and unvalidated messages is an important truth. Change is pervasive and ongoing, and so change management is one of the most important skills for any manager to have in a modern organisation. The organisation that manages change best is the one that will thrive most, and the managers that continuously succeed in implementing change will be among the most successful.

There are many books on change management, so why choose this one? Change can be very complex, and therefore it is easy to assume that change management has to be similarly complex. The challenge in defining a change management methodology is to have an approach that is simple and intuitive enough for all managers to apply immediately, yet comprehensive enough to meet the varied challenge of change. This book sets out to achieve this.

Change management can be a complicated and multifaceted subject, and whilst there is much navel gazing nonsense written about change, there is also significant value in some of the more complex studies of change and approaches to managing it. However, most managers do not have the luxury of becoming detailed experts in every single change tool and approach. This book describes a straightforward, structured and flexible approach that will improve organisational change in most situations. But it does not provide all the answers to every situation and you may find occasionally that you need to delve into more specialised approaches. However, by having a framework showing when you need more specialist approaches, any recourse to them can be done in a way that makes them readily applicable, rather than merely intellectually interesting.

This book aims to give you practical skills that you can apply immediately. It avoids interesting, but unhelpful, intellectual debates such as whether change is controllable or simply something that must be responded to. Fascinating for the academic, but for the manager in a real organisation facing real and immediate challenges, such issues are largely irrelevant.

This book is a sister volume to *Project Management: Step by Step* and adopts a similar format. Clearly, project and change management are separate disciplines dealing with different sorts of management challenges. However, there is huge value for a manager in understanding both project and change management. The books have been written as a pair, because projects often need the support of change management to ensure the deliverables are implemented, adopted and successful in the organisation. Equally, change initiatives often need to be supported by a project management approach in terms of structured planning, as well as task and progress management.

What you will be able to do once you have read the book

If you read this book, absorb and practise the approach described within it, and couple it with common sense, you will be able to:

- Assess and understand proposed changes and rapidly determine an approach to delivering them.

- Manage and deliver more complex changes than you can currently, with a reduced level of risk to your organisation.

- Feel more confident in, and even enjoy, the challenge of making change happen.

How to use this book

You can use this book in different ways. You may choose to sit and read it end to end, or simply to delve into the chapters that are most helpful to you. If you are facing, right now, a change challenge that you do not know how to overcome, I recommend that you go through the book twice. Firstly, rapidly scan it end to end to familiarise yourself with all the contents. Each chapter starts with a figure and two short sections titled 'this chapter covers' and 'the central point is'. You can do this scan in a few minutes, by simply reviewing the opening figure and reading these two sections, which are usually only one or two sentences. This will give you an end-to-end picture of the approach defined. Then read the book fully a second time to fill in the details in this picture, applying the components most relevant to your particular situation as you need to.

Each chapter covers one step of the change management approach, and is structured in the same way, with the following seven sections:

1. *This chapter covers*: gives a summary of the contents of the chapter.

2. *The central point is*: stresses the key idea(s) in the chapter.

3. *Setting the scene*: provides some context to the content of the chapter through one or more examples.

4. *Introduction to the chapter*: provides all the information you need to understand the activities you will perform in this chapter.

5. *The step-by-step guide*: the central part of each chapter provides core steps you must follow to complete this stage of your change.

6. *Key tips*: key points to remember from the chapter.

7. *To do now*: the immediate actions to undertake first to make the steps in this chapter a reality.

Your learning process as you read each chapter will be:

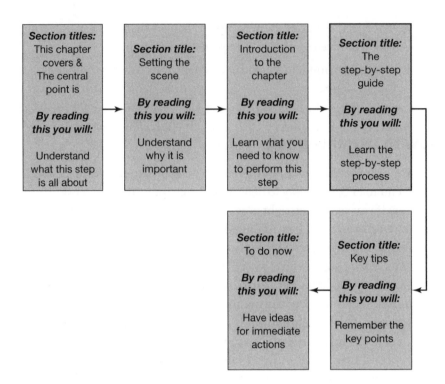

Acknowledgements

I would like to thank Anna Newton and Graham Jump for once again patiently reading drafts of this book and advising me how it could be improved and made more readable.

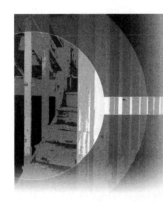

Step 1

Learn the basics

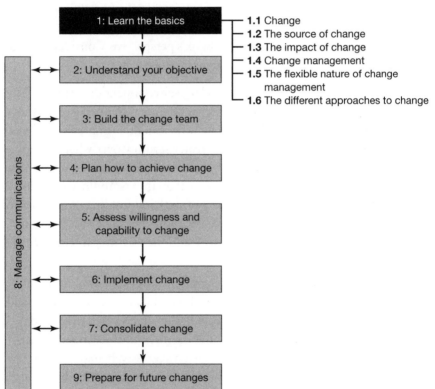

1: Learn the basics	**1.1** Change
	1.2 The source of change
	1.3 The impact of change
	1.4 Change management
2: Understand your objective	**1.5** The flexible nature of change management
	1.6 The different approaches to change

3: Build the change team

4: Plan how to achieve change

5: Assess willingness and capability to change

6: Implement change

7: Consolidate change

9: Prepare for future changes

8: Manage communications

- A short explanation of some of the fundamental concepts used in managing change which are core to utilising this book.

THE CENTRAL POINT IS:

- Change management is a discipline which can support an organisation in successfully transitioning from a sub-optimal current state to a desired future state.

Setting the scene

I use examples throughout the book, and begin each chapter with some to provide context. This chapter is specifically about defining 'change' and 'change management'. To assist, I start with some varied examples of what is meant by change from this book's perspective. Consider how you might approach the following change situations:

- You are a senior civil servant in a large government department. The service you provide to the country is coming into open gaze of the public and the national press. The work you do is in much greater demand, but there is also much greater scrutiny over what you do and how you do it. The general public want more from you, but they are increasingly critical of the way you do things. You have decided that you need to increase the level of staff and funding in key areas of your department. However, you also know that to be successful you must revise the way your staff work and the way they interact with the public and the media.

- You are the owner of a medium-sized business that has historically been quite profitable. You employ about 100 people, you understand your customers well and you provide a product which they need and for which historically there has been very little competition. Recently, a foreign business has started aggressively marketing a competing product to your customers. This is depressing both your sales volumes and your profit margins. You need to respond quickly, and you are starting to think through different ways of reacting. Perhaps you can cut costs to maintain your margins, or maybe you could improve your products or the surrounding services to maintain prices and demand.

- You are a new manager who has taken over a small team in a large multinational. The old manager ran the department apparently successfully for several years, and the team is a little complacent, at times even arrogant, about the service it provides to the rest of the business. You want to keep the high skills and quality of work the team does, but you think the team could be improved by being more customer focused, and having a lot more energy and motivation around what it does.

- You run the IT department in an organisation. You are about to install some new software on everyone's PC. The first part of your project, to develop the new software, was a great success. The work you have done so far is ahead of schedule and below budget, so you are feeling very pleased. However, you are concerned because the new software works in a very different way to previous versions and by installing it, you will be changing considerably the way people in the organisation have to work. Unless everyone understands and prepares for the new software in the correct way, the overall project will not be a success. You are not sure how to face this challenge.

All of these are examples of situations in which change needs to be made, and which would benefit from the application of a structured change management approach. Before getting into this, let's get a clearer understanding of what is really meant by the terms 'change' and 'change management'.

The step-by-step guide
STEP 1 – Learn the basics

Step 1.1 Change

In this book the word 'change' is really shorthand for *organisational change*. The organisation being changed can be a public company, privately owned business, government body, charity, or any other type of institution.

Change takes many forms: at one extreme, change can be about altering the reasons why an organisation exists and its core strategy; at the other, it may be about small revisions to a minor activity. Change can affect a whole organisation at once, or may be focused on a limited part of the organisation such as a single team. Typically, organisations are undertaking many changes in parallel all the time.

When a change is made, it is often to achieve one or more of the following:

- Enhanced processes and procedures.
- Improved IT systems.
- Amended infrastructure, such as new buildings or machinery.
- An innovative and broader range of products or services.
- Reduced cost of operations, or reduced cost to serve customers.
- Enhanced skills and capabilities of staff.
- Improved customer service.
- Changing organisational structure, which can include outsourcing.
- Revitalised culture of the organisation.
- A merger or de-merger between organisations.

This is not an exhaustive list, but it does cover many of the most common changes. Whatever the reason for it, an organisation wants to go from one state to another, and to do so it must change. Change is the process of transitioning from one state to another. Individual changes are normally referred to as a change project, a change programme or a change initiative. I use all of these terms in this book and do not differentiate between them.

Another word that is often used as a synonym for change is 'transformation'. Transformation, more fully called organisational or business transformation, usually relates to particularly complex and major change initiatives. In the business world there are a number of other terms used for specific types of change programmes, including cost reduction projects, cultural change initiatives and strategic improvement programmes. Most IT systems implementations are change projects as well, as they result in some degree of organisational change.

Step 1.2 The source of change

Change occurs as a response or reaction to some stimulus. The initial stimulus for change may be internal or external to an organisation.

Internally driven change comes about through the creativity of staff in an organisation generating an idea which has some benefit for the organisation. The change may be identified by the most senior management in an organisation (top-down change), but many good ideas come from lower levels in an organisational hierarchy (bottom-up change). By identifying new opportunities that can be achieved through change, organisations can improve and thrive.

Although there may be a constant stream of new ideas within the organisation, the truth is that change is most often motivated by a need to respond to some external stimulus. To respond successfully to an external stimulus requires both an awareness of what is happening externally and the insight to translate this into something meaningful for an organisation. Externally driven changes include:

- Responding to variations in competition, such as new entrants in a market, or competitors altering prices and introducing new products.
- Taking advantage of improvements in technology.
- Reacting to the varying demands and needs of customers.
- Preparing for new or altered legislation and regulation.
- Acting in response to more general trends in society, such as the move to healthier lifestyles, or the demand for more care of the environment.

Step 1.3 **The impact of change**

The term 'organisation' is one of those concepts that we all intuitively understand, but would probably define in very different ways. From a change perspective the important thing about an organisation is that it is made up of people. There may be many complexities involved in achieving any of the types of change described in the previous two sections of this chapter, but good experience, resources, technical skills, structure and logic would be enough to achieve them – if it was not for people. Change is challenging primarily because it involves many people and impacts upon many people.

Successful change requires adapting the way people work and behave, their skills and capabilities, and even their way of thinking and their attitudes.

People are not homogeneous; each individual has different levels of skills and capabilities, varying emotions and desires, diverse viewpoints and experiences. Predicting, understanding, planning and responding to the ways different people interpret and react to change is the core challenge in managing change.

Every individual will interpret and respond to any specific change in a different way. To understand this, consider a business which manufactures a range of products. When a change is made to introduce a new product the sales force may welcome it as it offers an opportunity to gain more sales commission by selling it to new customers. However, the sales force needs training and new sales materials, to understand the prices and discounts for the product, as well as how to sell it. The operational managers may be less welcoming, as the same product may make their lives more complex by giving them yet one more set of things to worry about in the factory they run. The billing department may be hardly affected, and only see this product as one new line to be put on customers' bills. The staff in the factory may not really be interested in the product itself, but perceive the change only through the ways they have to operate the new machinery brought in to manufacture this product. They may also be concerned about whether the new machines need as many people to operate as the existing ones, or whether new shifts will be introduced. The logistics department will think of the new product in terms of the supplies that have to be brought in to make the product, and how it will fit onto their lorries to be distributed.

Successfully launching this new product requires taking account of and managing all these different issues and viewpoints. To add to the complexity, within each group mentioned (sales, operational management, billing, factory staff, logistics), every individual will respond and adapt to the new product in different ways. Change management must prepare for different positive and negative reactions. Finally, to add yet another layer to this intricate puzzle, it is not just how individuals respond to the actual change occurring, people will respond in good and bad ways merely to the *suggestion* of change. So, change management has to predict and respond to people's reaction from the very outset when people in an organisation have only the very slightest notion that a change may be planned.

Throughout this book I refer to the people in an organisation undergoing change as 'staff'. This can be seen as a slightly old-fashioned word and in some situations even as negative. There are many alternatives, and I have worked with organisations that refer to the people working in them as employees, colleagues, associates, collaborators, partners, coworkers and so on. I have chosen to remain with the less fashionable term staff simply because it is a more generic and more widely understood word than the alternatives. The word 'staff' is meant in its traditional, positive way – as the combined group of people who keep an organisation going and who ensure it meets its objectives.

Step 1.4 Change management

Change management is the name for a disparate set of processes, tools, techniques, methods and approaches to achieve a desired end state through change. Change management is focused on the successful transition from one state to another.

Change management approaches have two fundamental goals:

- To help your organisation achieve its objectives which cannot be met with the current way you are organised, operate or serve your customers.

- To minimise the negative impact of any change. Well-designed and implemented change can lead to massive improvements in organisational performance, but after any change is made the organisation's performance tends to drop for a period of time before rising again. This drop in performance happens for a whole host of reasons and is discussed more in later chapters. (As a simple example of this phenomenon, when you upgrade your computer to a newer version of software, the newer version may let you do more things better and quicker, but just after you have loaded the software your performance tends to be worse until you get used to the way the new software works.) The second goal of change management is therefore to minimise the length of time and depth of this performance drop following any change.

This can be seen at a glance in a simple diagram. Figure 1.1 shows how the outcome in terms of operational performance levels may vary

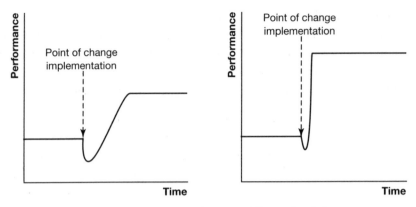

Figure 1.1 **The goals of change management**

depending on how well a change was managed. The outcome on the right is noticeably better than that on the left because:

- The final level of performance achieved is higher.
- The time to reach this level of performance is quicker.
- The drop in performance post-change is shorter and shallower.

Although 'change management' is a relatively mature piece of professional jargon there are many varied interpretations of the phrase. There are numerous people who profess some degree of change management expertise, and there are almost as many approaches to it. Yet all change management approaches are broadly about four things: clarifying what change is required; determining how to approach a change; implementing the change in the best way; and ensuring the change is successful.

Often, individual change management approaches focus on a specific aspect of change. For example, one approach may focus on the planning and logistics of change, almost like a project management methodology; another approach may focus on culture, human psychology and organisational behaviour; yet another may focus on the leadership skills required to deliver successful change; finally, an approach may focus on communications and overcoming resistance to change. This book provides a framework that brings together core elements from the key different approaches to change. As a short book it cannot cover all the richness and diversity of change management thinking, but by giving you a comprehensive framework it will allow you to understand change end to end and go deeper into more specialist approaches where required.

Well-known change management approaches include total quality management (TQM), re-engineering or business process re-engineering (BPR), lean, and Six Sigma. All of these are fundamentally about the same thing – driving beneficial change in organisations. Each of these approaches has influenced the way effective change management is done.

I end my definition of change management with a word of warning. When discussing change management with other professionals, make sure that they are actually talking about the same thing. In some contexts the phrase 'change management' has a related, but different, meaning from the one used in this book. It is unfortunate that this term is used to mean slightly different things to different professional groups, but you can at least minimise confusion by awareness and insisting on clarity. Common different usages of the term 'change management' include:

- Engineers (including IT professionals): change management in this case is the process of managing modifications to the specification of an engineered product, system, machine or process. For example, when an engineer makes an alteration to the specifications for a component of a machine he or she will check that this modification will still work in the way intended and still meets the requirements of the machine. This is controlled by a process called change management, change control or configuration management.

- Project managers: these also use the terms 'change management' or 'change control' to refer to the way they manage alterations to the scope or requirements of a project. Such changes may impact on the time a project takes, or the cost of a project, and they need to be assessed and formally accepted or rejected.

- Operational managers: change management is the way changes to an operational process or system are controlled to ensure that the change does not adversely affect operations. For example, if a new machine is to be installed on a production line in a factory, the change management process ensures, amongst other things, that this is not done until the machine is fully tested and found fit for purpose, that the change is made at the most appropriate time to minimise disruption to production, and that there is a contingency plan if the machine does not work properly and so operations can continue.

Step 1.5 The flexible nature of change management

The possible changes organisations need to undertake are infinitely varied, and the way they must be managed varies too. The way you would manage a modification to an IT system used in one department of a university would vary from the way you would manage moving the office location for a small charity. The approach to managing a reduction in the number of staff employed by a multinational company by 20% would differ from the way you would manage an alteration in business strategy for a chain of shops. The way people will respond to each of these changes, and the way the change must be managed, will vary significantly.

This is why good change management approaches are not a simple tick list methodology that can be applied in a template fashion exactly the same way in every situation. Good change management is a framework that must be tailored to the individual circumstances. This book provides an end-to-end approach to change management in a logical sequence. However, to apply change management successfully requires emphasising and altering each step more or less for each different change, and may even require you to juggle slightly the order of the steps. Deciding how to approach each individual change is part of a good change management process. Assessing the change and flexibly amending the change management approach accordingly is discussed in step 1.6 below, and further in the Appendix.

The change process in this book is shown as a linear process. This helps in planning as we tend to think of tasks in a linear sequence, where steps will be performed exactly in the order shown for a given situation. However, in reality change is often more complex and will require some jumping between tasks as appropriate in a specific situation. To do this successfully requires you to understand the whole process and not simply what you are doing at any one point in time.

Step 1.6 The different approaches to change

As already explained, there are an infinite variety of changes and a large number of change management methodologies. However, once you cut through the jargon of specific methodologies, there are essentially three main ways to approach change:

- As a project.
- With a task force.
- Embedded within operational processes.

Below I describe each of these in a little more detail. The Appendix, at the end of the book, provides more information on tailoring the approach in this book to different change situations. The approach described here is structured around change via projects, but most of the material is applicable to change through task forces and embedded within operational processes.

Change as a project

There are many definitions of the term 'project', but to me it is a simple and intuitive concept. A project is a task with a known end point. The first part of a project is agreeing the end point, or in project management terminology, 'the deliverables'. Once the deliverables are defined, the project works to develop them within an agreed time, cost, quality and scope. Project management is the structured methodology for delivering projects.

Not all projects are about organisational change, but many are. Projects are most useful in delivering change when it is driven by some form of development or has a very clearly defined end point. Good examples of project-driven change are the development and implementation of a new computer system, or the design, development and implementation of a new product. A merger and the subsequent post-merger integration is a change project. Alterations to facilities and office locations are change projects. Outsourcing part of your organisation is a change project.

In simple terms, change projects go through three main phases. Firstly, there is a start-up phase when the deliverables are agreed and resources are allocated for the project. Next comes a design and development phase when the deliverables are created. Finally, there is an implementation phase when the deliverables are applied to the organisation.

The approach to achieving change as a project requires a change team. This team, working outside of normal daily operations of the organisation, budgets and plans the change and identifies the deliverables. The deliverables are then created or developed. This development phase can take months or even years. Once the deliverables are ready, they are then implemented within the organisation. It is by implementing the deliverables that the organisation is changed in some way. The whole project must take change management into account and part of the development is planning and preparing for the change that happens in implementation, but it is during the implementation phase that change management is most obvious.

The approach defined in this book is structured around the model of change by project.

Change via task forces

A task force is a group of people, usually from the staff within your organisation, who are asked to focus on improving some aspect of performance. The difference between a task force and a project is not always obvious. Task forces can initiate projects, and projects may contain task forces. However, a project is defined in terms of a set of deliverables, which are intended to achieve a specific change objective. Once the deliverables are implemented, the project is complete. In contrast a task force is normally defined in terms of a performance improvement that has to be achieved in a certain time. Task forces are used typically for initiatives aimed at cross-functional improvements that do not require significant investment. Unlike a project, a task force may be ongoing, and regularly re-tasked with achieving ever increasing performance targets.

Task forces come under different names such as hit squads or performance improvement teams.

Consider the following examples to understand the difference between a project and a task force. A project is started to deliver a new IT system, which is intended to reduce costs. The project's objective is to reduce costs, but it has to do this by delivering the computer system. A task force is brought together to deliver a 10% reduction in customer complaints within six months. The task force has freedom as to how to achieve this outcome, but initially the task force members may not know how to achieve this.

Generally, the primary advantage of a task force is flexibility and rapid action. The primary advantage of a project is the very structured management of a complex series of tasks and the reduction of the associated risk of failure. The primary risk in task forces is that approaches may not be found to achieve the required performance improvement. The primary risks in projects are that the deliverables may not achieve the desired objective or the deliverables may not be created in the planned time or cost.

Task force members may work full time on the particular change, but normally the task force consists of staff who allocate a proportion of their time to the work. At task force meetings performance is analysed and suggestions for improvements are made. The task force members then implement the suggestions as part of their normal job role. Part of their personal performance goals are usually aligned to those of the task force.

Task forces are most useful in delivering inter-functional change where the end point is known, but the way to achieve it is not. Often there is not one factor causing the current levels of performance, but a complex interaction of many factors. Task forces help across organisational boundaries and bring people together to see how activity in one part of an organisation impacts on activity elsewhere.

Good examples of task-force-driven change are initiatives to decrease the number of faults in technology companies, and reducing the volume of customer complaints, or speeding up the cycle time for a specific business process for organisations in many sectors.

The approach defined in this book can be used to manage change via task forces, although step 4 (plan how to achieve change) is less relevant. The material in other steps, particularly steps 2 (understand your objective), 5 (assess willingness and capability to change), 7 (consolidate change), 8 (manage communications) and the Appendix (adapting the step-by-step approach), are directly relevant and will help in delivering change as a task force.

Embedded change

Embedded change can also be called continuous performance improvement. Embedded change is about staff performing their normal role, making ongoing adaptations to any component of their work and improving performance over time.

Embedded change requires staff to have the motivation, decision-making authority and capability to make changes in the way they work on a daily basis. Embedded change is closely associated with the ideas of quality management and empowered staff. Although the cumulative impact of embedded change can be huge, every individual modification is normally a small tweak to a process or procedure.

The lessons from this book can be used to support embedded change, although steps 3 (build change team) and 4 (plan how to achieve change) are less relevant. The material in other steps, particularly step 2 (understand your objective), 7 (consolidate change) and 9 (prepare for future changes), is directly relevant and will help in delivering embedded change.

Key tips

- Change, in the context of this book, is shorthand for organisational change.
- The core of change management is about managing people and their responses to change.
- The stimulus for change may be internal or external to an organisation.
- Every change is different, and the way it has to be managed needs to be tailored to this difference.
- Change can be delivered through projects, task forces, or the continuous adaptation of daily work.

TO DO NOW

- Identify what the source for your change is. Is it purely internally driven or is there an external stimulus?
- Think who will make good people to be involved in your change to ensure it is a success.
- Clarify what is unique about your change, and what is similar to previous changes you have undertaken.
- Review how your change is going to be delivered – as a project, via a task force, or as embedded change?

Step 2

Understand your objective

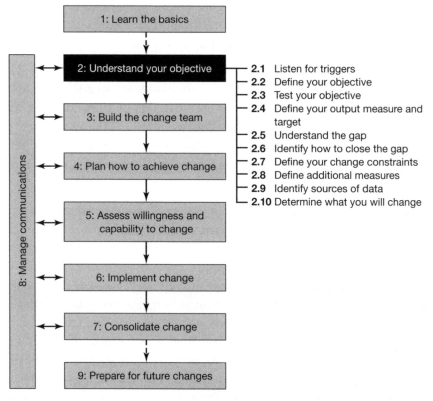

1: Learn the basics	

2: Understand your objective	2.1 Listen for triggers
	2.2 Define your objective
	2.3 Test your objective
	2.4 Define your output measure and target
3: Build the change team	2.5 Understand the gap
	2.6 Identify how to close the gap
	2.7 Define your change constraints
4: Plan how to achieve change	2.8 Define additional measures
	2.9 Identify sources of data
	2.10 Determine what you will change

5: Assess willingness and capability to change

6: Implement change

7: Consolidate change

9: Prepare for future changes

8: Manage communications

THIS CHAPTER COVERS:

- How to create the appropriate definition of the change you want to make, by defining and understanding your objective.

> ## THE CENTRAL POINT IS:
>
> - Whether your organisation needs a radical transformation, or a more modest adjustment, in order to achieve a successful outcome you must have a good understanding of your objective, and a definite, evidence-based, measurable way to achieve this objective.

Setting the scene

I start this chapter by considering the example of a business that wants to make changes. The example shows the need to understand clearly your objective before starting a change project.

The scenario is based on a business that is successful, with few visible threats to that success. Many companies in these conditions become complacent, but this is a far-sighted business that understands that great firms are equipped for the future. The organisation believes that now is the time to get ready for the world of tomorrow, and so decides to invest in a change programme to prepare for new competition and evolving customer needs.

This sounds like a worthwhile activity for a well-run enterprise wanting to protect its success in the longer term. Imagine you have just been given responsibility for this change programme. Are you sure your understanding of 'to prepare for new competition and evolving customer needs' is correct? What will you do to achieve this objective? You may think about improving products and services, or ways to reduce the costs of the business. Perhaps you would look at efficiencies you can gain in manufacturing products, or how to enhance the skills and competencies of the staff for yet-to-be-understood future challenges. You might start to rethink the whole ethos and business culture to be more forward thinking, or to focus more on customer services. Each of these is a laudable aim, but it's all a bit vague. To have an achievable goal you need to be able to convert worthwhile, but rather indistinct, intentions into defined activities. To do this you should be able to answer three questions:

- What is your objective? This should not be answered in terms of a broad intention, but as a specific, unambiguous and clear goal.

- How different is that from today? Unless you understand how your objective is different from today, you will not be able to determine the actions required for transition to that state.

- How will you know when you have achieved your objective? It is easy to assume you have achieved an objective because you have done some tasks, but to be really successful you need to have some way of measuring the impact of the actions you have taken.

Answering these three questions requires conversion of the broad intention, specified in our example as:

- Prepare for new competition and evolving customer needs

into a specific objective, such as:

- Develop a new range of products which will protect the company's revenues, margins and projected growth over the next 10 years

with a clear understanding of how that is different from now:

- All our products are mature and have had limited innovation over the last five years

and how you will measure success:

- Within three years 50% of our revenues will be generated from products which have been introduced in that period.

Now your change programme has a much clearer direction. Without direction, you can never be sure that the activities you want to perform will achieve your goals. In some situations direction comes from strategy work, and change management is often driven by strategy formulation. However, as well as strategic changes organisations make an ongoing series of smaller tactical adaptations and modifications. Such smaller changes are typically conceived by line managers in their day-to-day work. Small tactical changes should also be described with clear objectives.

A clear objective provides the basis to plan a change, and is also critical to good communications of, and gaining support for, the change. Poorly defined objectives will lead to dissipated and inefficient effort as people work on what they think is relevant to the change when in reality it is peripheral; at worst, poorly defined objectives will lead to completely wasted and futile work.

Once you know your objective you have two more activities to complete before you understand your change. The first is to assess the gap between this objective and your organisation's current position. The second is to identify what needs to change to fill this gap. Put more simply, to achieve your objective you need to know what has to change – an objective tells you where you want to get to, but not how to get there.

Let's look at a second example.

Think about a common problem in many organisations – low levels of customer satisfaction. In competitive and highly demanding markets customers not only want great products at reasonable prices, but also want excellent levels of service, and a first-rate customer experience. Imagine the situation in which a company has been tracking its levels of customer satisfaction through customer surveys, and the company has realised that it has a growing problem. There is a downward trend in customer satisfaction, and, worse, the levels of customer satisfaction achieved by this company are lower than those achieved by its key competitors.

In this situation, the company decides to embark on a transformation project to increase customer satisfaction. The objective is known, but what is the gap between the objective and the current state? Currently only 40% of customers regard this firm as giving good or excellent customer service and the management want to increase this to at least 80% of customers. Hence, the gap to be crossed is to increase the company's customer satisfaction rating by an additional 40%. So what can be done to fill this gap? Customer satisfaction is complex, and there are very many reasons for low levels of customer satisfaction. This business knows that all of the following issues contribute towards low customer satisfaction:

- Low product quality
- Relatively high product prices
- A sales force which regularly sells inappropriate products to customers
- Poor handling of customer queries
- Slow answering of calls in a call centre
- Lack of politeness by staff
- Billing errors, combined with complicated, unintelligible bills
- Poor fault fixing when products go wrong

- Ineffective complaint handling
- Slow delivery times and losses and breakages of goods in transit.

Every one of these issues in turn has many causes. For instance, poor fault fixing could be caused by ineffective fault diagnostics, negative staff attitudes when fixing faults, lack of resources allocated to resolving faults, poor staff skill levels, and so on.

Therefore, if your business needs to raise customer satisfaction, what are you going to do? Do you really understand all the factors that contribute towards your customers' dissatisfaction? Are you going to try and improve them all or are you going to focus your efforts and resources and fix the most major problems, or perhaps you will work to resolve the issues that are easiest and quickest to fix? Whichever you choose, you want to select an approach that efficiently and effectively meets your end goals. The change made must close the gap between the current level of customer satisfaction and the one wanted in an effective way. You should ask yourself:

- What are the causes of the gap between the current level of customer service and the level required?
- How can you compare or measure the impact of the different causes of the gap?
- Within the constraints and resources of your organisation, which causes can be resolved?
- Hence, what will you change to achieve the most effective improvement in customer service?

This chapter provides an approach to answer these questions.

Introduction to understanding your objectives

Successful change management starts by understanding *why* you want to change in terms of the objective you want to achieve. Unless you understand the objective you want to achieve you are unlikely to achieve it. Once you understand *why* you want to change, you are in a position to determine *what* needs to change to achieve this objective. The combined understanding of your objective and what you need to change to achieve this objective is the fundamental information required to plan and manage a change.

Understanding your objective, and what you need to change to achieve it, is not just required for planning the change: being able to communicate your objective clearly is essential in gaining management support, and driving a sense of urgency and commitment to the change. Without a clear objective, it is hard to get other members of the organisation to understand and give backing to the change you want to make. Beyond this, helping your organisation to understand what you will change is essential to encourage staff not only to have a commitment to the change, but to provide active and effective involvement in the work required to make the change happen. Later in this book you will be shown how important this support is.

The process to understand your change objective is explained fully in steps 2.1 to 2.10 of this chapter. The activities in this chapter are derived from four principles:

- An understanding of any change should be developed from a process of *structured analysis*, not from haphazard experimentation or impulsive unproven actions.
- Thinking about change is strengthened by gaining other people's views and allowing them to *challenge* your own thoughts.
- Good decisions about change are *evidence based*, and are not derived purely from assumptions or intuition.
- The best change plans combine knowledge from people at different levels in the organisational hierarchy and strike the correct balance between *top-down* and *bottom-up* thinking.

Let's discuss each of these in turn.

Structured analysis

Underlying every change is an objective you want to achieve. The objective is to transition from a current state to a future desired state. The change initiative you undertake is meant to close the gap between where you are and where you want to be. Closing the gap starts by identifying the most significant and the simplest factors causing the gap.

There is one very human problem with this approach. People often do not work in such a structured way, but jump from imprecise understandings of objectives to unproven conclusions about what causes current problems and incomplete views about what must be done to solve them.

This is perfectly normal, and even very senior and successful leaders in organisations are not immune from making decisions based on gut reaction. Your brain will often jump to solutions without fully understanding the problem that you need to resolve. There is nothing wrong with this, as long as you do not straight away assume the solutions you first think of are the ones you actually should implement. Intuition can be powerful, as long as it is used as a way to generate initial ideas, which are then tested and clarified. The way to be sure that the approach you take to your change is best is to go through a logical and structured process of analysis.

Structured analysis of change objectives, and what drives the gap between your current state and your desired state, is not about scientific levels of proof. But in making a change you expose your organisation to risk and you will use up your people's time and your organisation's money. If you are going to make a decision to expose your organisation to risk and cost, you should do this from a verified understanding that what you are doing is right, and this requires an appropriate level of rigour in thinking and analysis.

Challenged thinking

There are many changes you can make, and many different ways to approach every change. You want to select the best changes, and approach them in the optimal way. One important factor in achieving this is to ensure your thinking is exposed to robust challenge. Challenge comes when you share your ideas with other people, especially those whom you know have different viewpoints.

One of the biggest advantages of allowing challenge is to expose, clarify and potentially discard the assumptions that we all make day in and day out in our organisations. Unquestioned assumptions are one of the key limiting factors on achievements. Good challenge makes us all think through the assumptions we make, and often we find they are incorrect. Assumptions are useful as they enable us all to take efficient shortcuts without analysing everything we believe in every decision we make. But assumptions also constrain the breadth and creativity of thought. Freeing an organisation from assumptions that are no longer useful often leads to significant change opportunities and can be extremely productive.

Allowing your thinking to be challenged by others should not be seen as threatening, but as a way of strengthening ideas and plans. If a challenge is correct then you can adapt and improve your own ideas. If a challenge is incorrect, convincing the challenger of this is part of the process of gaining support for the change, and it will help you to refine the way you communicate about your change to overcome any future similar challenges. Challenge is help rather than hindrance.

The most robust thinking of all is that which has been exposed to a wide variety of challenges and shown to work whatever objection or suggestion is thrown at it.

Evidence-based decisions

An important part of this chapter is about the identification and collection of measures and measurement data. This section explains why this is so important.

Although change management can be complex, underlying it is a simple circle of activities that most managers will recognise: deciding what action to take, implementing the action, assessing the result of the action and, depending on the result, deciding the next action to take. Arguably, that is what management is about – making decisions and measuring results.

It's all too easy to make decisions based on unproven subjective criteria, anecdote, rumour, gut feelings and guesses, and to assess results based on the untested perception of outcome. Good managers seek to optimise both decision making and the assessment of results, and this means minimising the opportunity for subjectivity and ambiguity. The best decision making requires objective and reliable data, and the best assessment of results requires a way to unambiguous measurement of results. Whilst this principle is evident in much modern management practice, it is often forgotten when it comes to managing change.

Evidence in this context is made up of two parts: a measure and measurement data. A 'measure' is the definition of the scale that results can be measured against. The word 'measure', used as a noun and not a verb, is widespread in management, but is sometimes replaced by other terms such as 'key performance indicator' or KPI. There may be hundreds of different measures in a large organisation, and millions of pieces of measurement data collected every day. Measures may exist for every management activity. Examples of typical business measures include revenue, profitability, number of staff employed, levels of staff satisfaction, average sick days per employee, orders raised, customer complaints, average time to resolve a complaint, and so on.

To many readers this will be self-evident, and the way they are used to managing day to day. Unfortunately, when it comes to change the need for evidence in the form of agreed measures and reliable measurement data is, in my experience, usually forgotten. This happens because no one has taken the time to work out what the best measure is, or because data is not readily available and finding the data is seen as too much effort. Unless you are very lucky, designing changes without deciding how success is to be measured and collecting the supporting data will not achieve a good result. Organisations driving change without evidence can even end up with worse performance after the change.

Experience shows that whilst the time taken to select measures and to collect measurement data can initially slow down change initiatives, it will in the end speed you to more productive results by allowing you to focus on the real problems and not simply those you assume to be problems. But driving for evidence rather than anecdotal thinking does not mean ignoring intuition. Intuition is valuable, but it should be used to develop hypotheses that are researched, not simply to mandate untested ideas.

Making evidence-based decisions is all about how you monitor and assess a change based on facts. There are two key types of measures used in monitoring change:

- *Output measures*: an output measure is an assessment of the result of a change, and what it has achieved relative to your objective. An output measure provides a quantified evaluation of *what* a change has accomplished.

- *Input measures*: an input measure is an assessment of a factor that contributes towards achieving your objective (sometimes called a 'critical success factor' or CSF). An input measure is a quantified evaluation of *how* a change is being accomplished. There are normally many input measures for every output measure.

The distinction between input and output measures may seem a pedantic detail, but it is important to understand the difference to get the most from this chapter. Think about a change to increase a business's profits. For such a change the output measure is the level of profitability in pounds. The input measures are gauges of the factors that contribute towards profitability, such as the number of units of products sold, the price per unit achieved, the operating costs, etc.

If your change is to decrease the amount of floor space an organisation leases the output measure is square metres of office space leased, and input measures could be the number of staff you have, the average floor area per member of staff, the percentage of time staff are in the office, etc. The identification of appropriate input and output measures, and the collection of data to evaluate the measure, is core to this step.

Top-down vs bottom-up

The final principle is to find the correct balance between top-down and bottom-up thinking. By top-down I mean thinking that is done at the top of an organisational hierarchy by the leadership team, executives and senior management. By bottom-up I mean thinking that is done at the lower levels of an organisational hierarchy by staff in any role. Good change thinking, design, planning and implementation use a combination of top-down and bottom-up thinking. Although it varies from organisation to organisation, typically people at the top of an organisational hierarchy have a stronger view of overall strategy and are often better at defining the objective from a change process. People at other levels in an organisation tend to have a more realistic understanding of the actual workings of the organisation and the nature of interactions with customers and other key stakeholders, and understand what is currently effective and what is not working properly. Therefore, they are often best at defining what needs to change to achieve an objective. It is only by combining the knowledge from all levels that an organisation can be sure it is undertaking the optimal change.

Pure bottom-up-driven change risks being irrelevant to the future direction of an organisation and should be checked against top-down views and strategy. Pure top-down-driven change is often impractical and unimplementable. The optimal balance between top-down and bottom-up thinking varies from situation to situation, but rarely does good change result without both.

In determining the objective of every change and converting this into an understanding of what needs to be modified, your aim must be to get the best combination of knowledge, ideas and experiences from all levels of an organisation.

Note – the order of step 2 and step 3

A judgement needs to be made on the order of step 2 (this step), and step 3 (build the change team). Sometimes steps 2 and 3 will need to occur in parallel, rather than sequentially as the order of the book indicates. This is discussed further in the Appendix.

The step-by-step guide
STEP 2 – Understand your objective

Step 2.1 Listen for triggers

The first part of change is the most inexact as it is about capturing the ideas you have on a daily basis. Any change process starts with an idea. This idea is the trigger for change. Great ideas will be occurring all the time in your organisation. The difficulty in most organisations is not an individual having an idea, but those ideas being captured by someone with the interest, power or drive to make the change happen.

Examples of triggers for change can be best shown as the observations, thoughts, statements and questions that arise in everyday conversations in organisations, as shown in the list below:

- The government is looking to reduce costs. Does this pose a risk to our funding?
- My mother says she does not understand our bill. Is this typical of our customers?
- A new competitor has entered our market. What should we do?

- Office space is getting more expensive to lease. How should we control our costs?
- I have seen some great new products in the market from our competitors. How should we respond?
- I have overheard a lot of staff moaning about this organisation as a place to work. Do we need to do anything?
- Our customer satisfaction measures are terrible. What can we do?
- We seem to lose an awful lot of orders. Is there something wrong?

There are many sources of ideas. For example, change may be triggered:

- *As an outcome from strategy work*: how to develop a strategy is outside the scope of this book, but the output from strategy is important. Change objectives are produced as part of strategy development. Arguably, the main purpose of strategy is to define what changes an organisation must make and their relative priority.
- *From the analysis of feedback from stakeholders* (customers, team members, peers and other stakeholders): this may be positive feedback and suggestions, but often it is about working through negative feedback in the form of trends in complaints and faults.
- *From market research*: market research, about your organisation's or competitors' brands, services, products and other customer views, is a great source of potential change ideas. All organisations benefit by understanding and responding to their real customer needs.
- *As a directive*: executives, business owners, funding bodies, or in the case of public sector groups, the government, simply tell you to change. This is not always an ideal starting point, but it would be naïve to think that it does not happen!
- *From the observation of performance*: for metric-led organisations that have effective measures of performance and target levels to achieve, a frequent stimulus to change is failure to meet performance targets. This is often a good way to identify very specific and focused change initiatives.
- *From the insight of a member of an organisation*: occasionally someone has a truly creative insight about the potential for change. This is not that common as most ideas for change tend to come about through external pressure and triggers, but it does happen.

One difficulty is that unless the idea comes from someone senior in an organisation, it is often not heard or listened to. Having mechanisms to capture and review ideas will widen an organisation's access to creative insights – whether it is as simple as a suggestion box, through to regular sessions where senior managers listen to the views and ideas of other staff.

- *From brainstorming and other idea generation sessions*: formal and deliberate processes for generating ideas and for spurring creativity can generate many productive change ideas. (Brainstorming is popular and well known, but there are other idea-generating techniques, some of which are also simple but more powerful.) Organisations that regularly invest time in allowing staff to generate ideas, and even train them in intentional creative approaches, often have a strong pool of original initiatives to call upon.

- *From the day-to-day experiences of senior managers*: this arises from managers and executives listening to, overhearing, observing or reading something that triggers alarm bells in their heads. It can be as simple as talking to friends or relatives, overhearing a conversation in the staff canteen or lift, or reading an article in the press. This is a surprisingly common source of change triggers.

Triggers like these will produce a need to change or a broad idea for a change, but typically do not in themselves produce a well-defined change objective.

Step 2.2 Define your objective

The next step is to convert from a general idea for change into a clear objective. Producing a well-defined objective takes effort, and starts by having an awareness of what a good objective looks like. A good point to hold in mind is that an objective is not merely a set of words you will use at the start of your work – it is a tool that you will use and refer to throughout the change. The better a tool fits your needs, the easier your work will be.

The objective is a description of what it is you want to achieve by undertaking your change. Ensuring that you have a clear objective makes certain that you really know where your change initiative will lead to.

If you cannot define your objective then you risk wasted effort, and without a defined objective there is a significant chance that the various people who will be involved in a change will be working towards different end points.

The objective needs to be a simple statement that everyone who will be involved in the change can understand. Ideally it is expressed in a single sentence or at most one paragraph of text. Examples of good, simple change objectives are shown in Table 2.1.

One way to think of an objective is as the compass for your change initiative. A properly operating compass gives clear direction, but a poorly functioning compass is more of a hindrance than a help. A properly constructed objective is:

- *Correct*: it may sound obvious, but any objective must be correct. When you read the objective does it really say what you want it to say? If you are unsure spend some more time defining it. The effort you spend now on getting it right will be repaid later on. Now is the time to be pedantic and precise; a sloppily worded objective will result in unfocused and irrelevant effort somewhere in your organisation.

You want a compass that, when it says it is pointing north, it really is pointing exactly north.

Example objectives for different change initiatives
1 To reduce our dependence on government funding
2 To increase the level of customer service we achieve
3 To reduce the amount of office space we lease
4 To develop the skills and competencies of our staff to be able to handle the future challenges and changes facing the business
5 To refresh our product set with new, innovative products
6 To change our culture and environment to be a more enjoyable organisation to work in
7 To improve the quality of orders processed

Table 2.1 **Example change objectives**

- *Clear*: it is no good defining an objective people cannot understand. Your objective must be clear and easy to understand.

  Your compass needs to be easy to read and to use.

- *Meaningful*: being really clear is not just about being linguistically and grammatically correct, but also that your objective is phrased in a way that members of the organisation will understand. Often, the whole point of a change is to alter the way an organisation acts and thinks, but even so the objective needs to be phrased in a way that the staff in the organisation will relate to. If you are in a conservative organisation, specifying change in the latest street slang or business school jargon will not result in ready acceptance by the people in the organisation. If you are an academic body, then couching a change objective purely in business terminology will not be helpful. Similarly, specifying a change in a business in precise, but typically complex, academic language is unlikely to be readily meaningful to this audience.

  The points on your compass need to be readily identifiable as N, S, E and W and not some arcane or unfamiliar symbols that you have to concentrate on and interpret every time you look at them.

- *Unambiguous*: it is difficult to be absolutely unambiguous, but you should seek to be as unambiguous as possible. The reason you are defining your objective is to give direction to your change initiative. If your objective is ambiguous then you have not given sufficient direction to a change.

  It's no good having a compass that two people read differently depending on their personal interpretation. When the compass points west everyone should read it as pointing west.

- *Concise*: a good objective needs to be quick to explain, easy to remember and easy to apply. If it takes more than a few seconds to explain a change objective you will not easily gain understanding or support, and you will inhibit its flow through the organisation.

  A quick glance at the compass should be sufficient to check the direction you are going in.

This list is really about language and the words you use to specify your objectives, but what about the nature of the objective itself? The key characteristic of good objectives is that it is challenging, but achievable. If you want to get the best from your organisation every change should challenge the organisation. We all achieve our best when we set ourselves challenges, but they must be realistic and achievable.

So how do you move from the trigger to a well-defined change objective? There is no single right approach, but the following five activities provide a simple way to develop an objective:

- *Discuss*: when you have an idea or a set of ideas, discuss them with other people in the organisation to flesh out and clarify them. Discuss the ideas with people with different views to ensure they get plenty of challenges.

- *Document*: write the idea down in the form of an objective. Many ideas seem clear in our minds, but it is only when we write them down that we are forced to be correct, clear and concise. If you find as you document your objective that you have to write more than a few lines, it is not clear enough. Make sure that every word in the sentence(s) is the right choice.

- *Review*: review yourself and get feedback from as many people as you can. Ask people if they know what it means, and check that what they say matches what you want to say. Is it meaningful and unambiguous?

- *Amend*: take the feedback you have received and produce a revised, documented version of the objective.

- *Finalise*: make an explicit statement that the objective is agreed and distribute it to other involved people.

This may initially seem like overkill. After all, isn't your objective just a sentence, and aren't sentences easy to write? Yes, but you are not trying to write any sentence! You are writing the sentence that really defines the objective. Errors, ambiguities, confusion and inaccuracies will magnify as your change progresses. The less tangible the change, the more specific the objective definition needs to be. Getting the objective right is essential. Following a compass bearing requires accuracy, and the further you are going, the more accurate you must be. Walking on a bearing of 70° may not feel much different from walking at 75°, but two people following each of these bearings will soon be in quite different places.

Step 2.3 Test your objective

When you have defined your objective test it against three straightforward questions:

- Is this an important change?
- What will the impact of this change be on your customers or other stakeholders?
- Is the change achievable?

At this stage you may not be in a position to give detailed or robust answers to these questions – don't worry! You will work through these questions in an exhaustive way as you work through later steps in this book. However, take a short period to reflect on these questions now.

Is it an important change?

The purpose of the first question is a quick common-sense check that achieving the objective you have specified is worthwhile. In many organisations the problem is not defining ideas for changes, but prioritising between them. There is always more that could be achieved than can be done with the available time and resources. So, if you could solve only one issue in your organisation, would it be this one? If not, how important is it? Before you go any further you need to believe that the change you are about to embark on is going to be worth the possible cost, disruption and risk it will expose your organisation to. If you do not honestly think the change is worthwhile – stop now.

What will the impact of this change be?

The purpose of the second question is to ensure that the change you are about to embark on is actually good for the organisation (and not just good for you or someone else in the organisation). Will this change have any impact on your final customers or other stakeholders? When the change is complete, will you be able to operate more cheaply, more effectively, with better service levels, or to a larger customer group, etc.? Will your customers benefit in some way when this change is made? If the answer is 'no' to all questions of this type – why are you bothering?

Is the change achievable?

The purpose of the final question is to ensure that you are not being too ambitious. Too much ambition can make you bite off more than you can chew. Change management professionals often talk of initiatives which try to 'solve world hunger'. Unquestionably, solving world hunger would be a great objective, but it is unrealistic to assume that you will achieve it in one project. There are countless examples of change projects that have flopped even though they started out with great intentions and passion to achieve them, but simply were too big to achieve. Any change project you undertake needs to be manageable and achievable. You will do more for your organisation by delivering ambitious, but realistic, achievements than gallantly failing on wildly optimistic ideas. This requires judgement. If you are too cautious you will miss the opportunity for dramatic improvement that change often offers. If you are too ambitious you will simply waste time and resources trying to achieve the unachievable. If you are unsure, seek some advice from an experienced change professional who has seen radical change achieved.

Step 2.4 Define your output measure and target

To make your objective an achievable goal, it needs to be supported with the most appropriate measure of success – or output measure. Your output measure is the mechanism which tells you when your objective has been achieved. By collecting the relevant measurement data you will know how much you have achieved, how much more needs to be achieved, and when you have reached your destination.

You may think that there are many ways your objective can be measured, but in reality there is normally one fundamental measure of success for any change. What is the primary thing you will achieve with your change? What is the result you are trying to achieve, and how is this result best measured? If your answer to this question is a long statement with the word 'and' many times, then you do not really have a single change initiative, but many. Well-designed change initiatives will usually be capable of achieving multiple benefits, but you should always strive for a primary way in which you will measure success. Occasionally, there really are several measures of success. However, if you think you have multiple output measures check with yourself that you are not including input measures (see the introduction above or step 2.10 below), and that you are not simply indulging in unclear or lazy thinking. If you have defined your change objective clearly, your output measure should be fairly obvious.

The output measure you choose should be defined in terms of both the units you will measure and the target level (or result) you want to achieve against this measure. Defining the target you want to achieve is beyond the scope of this book. Targets are normally defined as part of your organisation's performance management framework, although for a simple change they may be defined from the judgement of the change sponsor.

Table 2.2 shows some examples of the output measures and targets for the changes described previously in Table 2.1.

If your change initiative's output measure is not obvious, don't just plump for the first measure that comes into your head. There is a common management saying, 'what you measure is what you will get', that should always be borne in mind. If you choose a different measure, you will tend to achieve different results.

For example, a company that is making changes to increase profits is looking for the most appropriate measure to track. The most obvious output measure is profit levels, but organisations often miss measuring the obvious! So what else might be measured? If we ignore the complexities that accounting creates, profit is dependent on the costs to run your business, the amount you sell, and the price you get for every item sold. So, you might think that a change initiative focused on achieving any one of decreased costs, increased sales volume or increasing prices will increase profits. As Table 2.3 shows, it might, but then again it might not!

Change objectives	Output measure	Target
1 To reduce our dependence on government funding	Percentage of funding from non-governmental sources	To have 25% of funding from sources other than the government (e.g. private sector)
2 To increase the level of customer service we achieve	Percentage of customers who rate us as good or very good for service	For at least 90% of our customers to rate us as good or very good for service
3 To reduce the amount of office space we lease	Amount of office space in square metres	To decrease the amount of office space we lease by 25%
4 To develop the skills and competencies of our staff to be able to handle the future challenges and changes facing the business	Percentage of change initiatives which achieve their business case	To achieve 100% success rate in change initiatives we undertake
5 To refresh our product set with new, innovative products	Revenues generated by new products	To generate revenues of at least £5m from new products
6 To change our culture and environment to be a more enjoyable organisation to work in	Percentage of staff satisfied with our business	For at least 75% of our staff to regard our organisation as an enjoyable place to work
7 To improve the quality of orders processed	Percentage of orders processed correctly Percentage of orders rejected	For 100% of order forms to be processed correctly, and for a maximum of 5% of orders to be rejected due to being incomplete or poorly filled in

Table 2.2 **Example measure of success**

Output measure	Impact of this measure
Lower cost	You will tend to choose change activities that will lower costs. This is fine if your objective was to minimise costs, but in measuring costs you will tend to ignore any opportunity that increases costs but which also increases profitability by greater sales or higher prices. Transformation programmes are often focused on cost cutting and are sometimes successful. However, many organisations have embarked on cost cutting but lost sight of the opportunity to grow through investment. The price of a lower cost base is sometimes a much smaller business
Increased sales volume	You will tend to choose change activities that will increase sales volume. This would work if your objective was to increase sales volume, but in focusing on sales volume you may actually decrease profits as you seek any sale you can get, even those that are unprofitable. Many organisations have experienced the situation of encouraging sales forces to increase sales volumes at any cost, only to find that whilst revenues may increase the business ends up with lots of unprofitable customers and overall profitability declines
Higher price	You will tend to choose change activities that will increase prices. This could be perfect if your objective was to maximise prices. However, if you raise your prices too high you may still make some sales, and the profit per sale may be higher, but you risk losing many sales to customers who are only interested in paying a lower price. Unless the additional profits per sale are bigger than the loss in profits from lost sales, you are actually worse off
Increased profitability	This is ideal. It may be more complex to measure, but it will tend to force you to assess any change in terms of profit and profit margins, which is what you have actually set out to achieve

Table 2.3 **Impact on activity of different measures**

Lower costs, higher prices or greater sales are each contributory factors towards greater profitability, but improving any one alone will not guarantee greater profitability. This may seem self-evident, but there are countless examples of change initiatives that have started without the most appropriate measure of success. The initiative's success is measured against an input measure, and not the real fundamental measure of success. Because this is done the change programme focuses on the input measure alone, and the programme may achieve improvements against this measure, but at the cost of failing to achieve the overall objective.

A final cautionary note – the output measure you select should not be simply chosen because it is something you already measure.

Step 2.5 Understand the gap

The purpose of a change initiative is to move your organisation to a state in which it meets your objective. To achieve this requires transitioning between where you are and where you want to be; the difference between the two is a gap. The simple question to ask yourself is: what is the difference between this objective and what happens now? The answer to this question is your gap.

Again, as in defining an objective, be precise in defining your gap. If you underestimate the gap your change initiative risks not achieving your objective. If you overestimate the gap, you may deliver more than you intended, but also you may end up trying to achieve an unachievable or spend more money or time than necessary.

Your gap should be related to the output measure and target (Table 2.4).

Now you know the gap you will start to get an intuitive idea of whether your change project is going to be a major transformation or a simpler modification. For example, to go from a 70% staff satisfaction rating to 75% seems an achievable goal with some minor modifications, whereas going from a customer satisfaction rating of 40% to 90% is likely to require a more fundamental change in attitudes and approaches.

Change objectives	Target	Current status – gap to be filled
1 To reduce our dependence on government funding	To have 25% of funding from sources other than the government (e.g. private sector)	0% currently – gap is 25%
2 To increase the level of customer service we achieve	For at least 90% of our customers to rate us as good or very good for service	According to our monthly customer survey, 40% of existing customers rate us as good or very good; we therefore need to increase this by 50%
3 To reduce the amount of office space we lease	To decrease the amount of office space we require by 25%	We currently lease approximately 6000 m^2 of office space. We need to reduce the amount we lease by 1500 m^2
4 To develop the skills and competencies of our staff to be able to handle the future challenges and changes facing the business	To achieve 100% success rate in change initiatives we undertake	Currently we do not really know how many change initiatives we undertake and how many are successful. The gut feeling is that we are very poor
5 To refresh our product set with new, innovative products	To generate revenues of at least £5m from new products	We currently generate £100k of revenues from products introduced in the last 2 years. We need to increase this by 4900% to get to £5m
6 To change our culture and environment to be a more enjoyable organisation to work in	For at least 75% of our staff to regard our organisation as an enjoyable place to work	According to our quarterly staff satisfaction survey, currently 70% of staff regard our organisation as an enjoyable place to work. We must increase this by a further 5% to hit our targets
7 To improve the quality of orders processed	For 100% of order forms to be processed correctly, and for a maximum of 5% of orders to be rejected due to being incomplete or poorly filled in	Currently unknown until we start measuring. However, anecdotally about 20% of orders are rejected, and a similar number incorrectly processed

Table 2.4 **Example gap statements**

Step 2.6 Identify how to close the gap

When you know the gap to be filled you next need to identify what could close the gap. One way to consider is by overcoming problems which inhibit your current performance. Another way is by identifying ways to do things differently or otherwise to take advantage of new approaches to performing work.

Whether your gap can be overcome by solving problems or by new approaches, you can consider both as opportunities for change. You must first collect ideas for opportunities for change, which can come from:

- *Discussion forums*: inside your organisation, or with customers and external stakeholders. Asking simple questions such as what can be done better will generate many ideas for change.

- *Brainstorming sessions*: with your staff and managers. Often, for major change ideas, experienced non-executives have many great ideas.

- *Analysis of work*: observation and formal assessments of individuals and teams at work. A good way to do this is to follow a transaction around the business. For example, if you are studying orders, literally follow an individual order through the business and see how people work on it. This can be very enlightening, and often gives a fuller understanding than simply asking people to explain what happens. Frequently, if staff are asked to explain processes they describe how they should work, or how they think they work – but not how they actually work. Observing work in action provides a better understanding of how processes really work.

- *Customer and staff interviews*: more structured and in-depth reviews with smaller groups of people than a discussion forum.

- *Research*: formal research or advice from academics or other specialists.

- *Subject matter expert's advice*: specialists such as consultants, academics or, if you have them, in-house experts who have experience of other organisations or teams with similar issues and can bring best practice ideas.

Let's explore one of these in a little more detail. A straightforward way to start the identification of opportunities for change is by running a brainstorming session. This session is ideally run by an impartial and expert facilitator. It should involve a range of people who understand the area, and ideally some external support from consultants or other subject matter experts.

Run through the following steps:

- Select the attendees, choosing a balanced group of people with an interest in and knowledge of the area.

- Brief the attendees in advance of the meeting and ask them to think about the reasons why current performance is what it is, and what can be done to improve it. This is best achieved by preparing some briefing materials outlining the objective of the change initiative and the purpose of the brainstorm to generate ideas of opportunities to achieve this objective (both by overcoming existing problems and seizing new opportunities). Be clear that the attendees should be thinking about what are problems with the existing situation, but also what opportunities can be applied to the existing situation.

- Run the brainstorm session.

- After the session resolve any issues that arose and collect further information as required.

- Document the proposed opportunities for change.

- Reconvene the group and discuss each opportunity. This is not to filter any ideas but to ensure they are commonly understood and correctly documented.

Continuing with the examples I have built up in the previous steps of this chapter, you might generate the list of opportunities in Table 2.5 for change (in real life I would expect you to generate more opportunities than this).

	Change objective	Possible causes of the gap/opportunities for change
1	To reduce our dependence on government funding	We have never sought external funding before We are unknown to most possible private sector funding bodies We have no relationships with the private sector or anyone else who might fund us except for the government Apart from the government no one would perceive any reason to fund us
2	To increase the level of customer service we achieve	Low product quality Reduce high product prices A sales force which regularly sells inappropriate products to customers Poor handling of customer queries Slow answering of calls in a call centre Lack of politeness by staff Billing errors, combined with complicated, unintelligible bills Poor fault fixing Ineffective complaint handling Slow delivery times and losses and breakages of goods in transit Poorly located stores Brand associated with cheap, shoddy products
3	To reduce the amount of office space we lease	We have too many staff We have too much space per member of staff We have too much ancillary space in the offices, e.g. meeting rooms and storage People spend too much time in the office when they should be elsewhere (with clients etc.) There is no hot-desking or home-working We do not own our own property
4	To develop the skills and competencies of our staff to be able to handle the future challenges and changes facing the business	Our staff have a lack of training in change management Our staff have a lack of experience in change management There is no encouragement or reward for having these skills We have the wrong profile of people to manage change We have no change management roles There is a lack of sponsorship for these skills at a senior level Poor experiences of previous changes and equating change with redundancy

Change objective	Possible causes of the gap/opportunities for change
5 To refresh our product set with new, innovative products	We have had a limited range of new products The products we have had have been poorly understood by sales The new products have a lower sales commission than the old ones and so are not pushed by sales The new products are not popular with our broad customer base and have only appealed to narrow niches There is much greater competition and lower prices for our new products. We have to sell many more units to achieve the same revenues
6 To change our culture and environment to be a more enjoyable organisation to work in	We have had a very high cost reduction focus There have been many redundancies and continuing uncertainty The office space is a poor environment to work in Senior management are perceived to be indifferent and uncaring to staff, only being interested in financial targets Staff perceive that we invest little in training or education compared with competitors There is seen to be little chance for advancement or earning more money We pay at the rate of the bottom 25% of organisations and benefits beyond salary are limited
7 To improve the quality of orders processed	Sales force under pressure, having too little time to do a quality job on the order form Lack of care by sales force as no incentive to get order forms right Badly designed and ambiguous forms Complex form which takes a long time to complete, with too much repeat information Lack of use of modern technology to enhance process Low skills in order processing teams

Table 2.5 **Sample gap causes**

What I have described is a very simple way to identify opportunities for change. More complex and specialised change methodologies sometimes have more powerful, but also more complex, approaches to identifying opportunities for change. In some cases describing these approaches would take a longer book than this! If the way I have defined does not generate a good enough understanding of the opportunities for change it is worth doing more research into the more complex methods. The remainder of this step (2.6) is optional and gives some indicative pointers to these approaches.

Techniques for identifying opportunities for change

The following subsection provides additional material for step 2.6. To continue with the process you can jump straight to step 2.7 and reference this material later.

Many change management methodologies contain extensive ways for identifying opportunities for change. This subsection provides information to enable you to research these methodologies.

Traditionally, the way to improve a process or system is to look for the points where things go wrong. The starting point is to ask simply 'why is this going wrong?' Such an approach tends to be driven by the knowledge that something is amiss, or because an organisation is not hitting a particular performance target. Techniques such as *root cause analysis* will then try to determine, from a complex set of possible interactions, what actually is the main root cause and target action to solve this specific issue. Applying analysis approaches such as *Kaizan* can be very powerful in understanding root causes. If techniques such as *systems dynamics* are also applied, root cause analysis can develop a really good understanding of the primary weaknesses in a process or system and where it can be improved.

One key systems dynamics concept is that of *leverage points*. Instead of looking at a problem having a number of separate root causes, systems dynamics shows how to look at the causes as a series of interdependent variables which act as an integrated system to produce a result. A leverage point is one variable that can be changed, which has a positive impact on other variables and starts a positive virtuous circle of interactions. For example, consider that your objective is to improve customer service by improving the way you deal with customer faults. One solution may be to improve your fault handling processes. A better leverage point would be to improve the quality of your products so you get fewer faults in the first place. This has leverage because it directly decreases fault rates, it also means that the staff dealing with faults have fewer faults to handle and so can do a better job on the remainder, and it will increase customer satisfaction in other ways. Consider a different example: you are trying to reduce the amount of office space your organisation uses. One solution could be to decrease the size of everyone's desk. A better leverage point is to increase home-working. This not only reduces the amount of office space you need for staff to work by actually reducing the number of staff in the office, but has an impact in other areas. Home-working will reduce the number of meeting rooms you need as people switch from face-to-face meetings to conference calls, it will decrease the amount of parking space you require, the size of the canteen needed, and additionally it can improve staff satisfaction. Finally, once some people start home-working, more tend to follow.

There are disadvantages to relying solely on techniques like root cause analysis. By focusing on what is wrong with a process one is predisposed to negative thinking and it also tends to miss out on the good points of current working practice. Sometimes a more helpful approach is to try and find what is actually right about a way of working and build on this. *Appreciative enquiry* specifically starts by asking people to think about what is good and what they enjoy about work. By asking people to think about the positive aspects this approach helps people to expand on current good practice, and develops a very positive mindset.

Really experienced change management practitioners will apply a range of techniques to identify opportunities for change. Practitioners may start with a technique like appreciative enquiry as it can generate great interaction between people and understanding of different roles in processes which in itself can develop significant improvements in performance. On top of this a positive frame of mind is very helpful when looking for creative and innovative ways to improve performance. However, to optimise performance really it is usually necessary to do some root cause analysis, ideally using a structured and measured analysis, as is required in Six Sigma.

Six Sigma and *lean* methodologies look at problems from another angle, by making detailed assessments of processes. The two methods were originally developed separately in manufacturing, but increasingly they are merging and have been applied to organisations in a wide range of sectors, including the public sector. These techniques seek to remove complexity and non-value-adding tasks from all processes, and look to ensure that processes operate in a consistent way and with a measurable and known tolerance. Typically, in reviewing processes, handovers between different people working on the process are clarified, simplified and reduced. Six Sigma shows how the most efficient and effective processes operate consistently to a very limited tolerance with few or no tasks that do not add value to the final outcome. Six Sigma looks for variations in tolerances, and then tries to remove them. Lean methodology looks to minimise process cycle time and remove non-value-adding tasks. Six Sigma requires significant effort and skill in collecting and analysing data, but can lead to major performance improvements.

Step 2.7 Define your change constraints

All organisations operate in an environment of constraints. Even the most well-funded or profitable organisation has limits to the money and time it can invest in any activity. There may be other constraints that are specific to your individual situation.

The constraints that you operate under need to be understood for two reasons. Firstly, it will help you plan your change. If your change must be completed in three months, then anything to close a gap that will take more than three months is obviously irrelevant to your initiative. Secondly, understanding your constraints is useful to enable you to select and prioritise between different approaches to change. In a change programme in which your objective is to improve your offices, if you are unconstrained in time you may choose to move or build a new office, but if you must achieve some of your objective in six months then it is more realistic to redecorate your existing offices. Similarly, if your change programme is to achieve improved order processing and you have a large budget you may choose to implement a new automated system, whereas if your budget is severely constrained you may prefer to update and improve your paper-based order forms.

To determine your constraints you should ask questions such as:

- Do you have any time constraints? Do you need to change quickly, or even in a specific time frame (is there some event which you must have changed in a certain time)? Alternatively, do you have the luxury of a longer time to achieve your objective?
- Do you need to change cheaply or using limited resources, or to a predefined fixed budget?
- Are there any strategic constraints?

- Are there any operational constraints?
- Are there any legal, regulatory or ethical constraints?
- Are there any other customer constraints?
- Are there any other stakeholder constraints?
- Are there any temporary or tactical constraints?

You should be aware that senior managers in most organisations are always under pressure to do things quickly and cheaply. So, when identifying constraints it is important to differentiate between desires or preferences and real constraints. Any constraint you accept will limit your options – and therefore if budget or time is being proposed as a constraint it should only be accepted if it really is a constraint and not simply a preference.

You need to apply judgement in identifying your constraints. Do not use constraints to be overly conservative or ignore unusual, creative, aspirational or demanding objectives. Do not give yourself artificial constraints, or use constraints as a premeditated excuse for not following a particular course of action – and watch for others doing this. The purpose of identifying constraints is not to stop you making a decision to undertake difficult or unpopular change, it is so you understand the real limits and do not embark on a change programme that is truly pointless, or is honestly beyond your capabilities, means or the situation you work in.

Many constraints will be about the rules and assumptions on which your organisation operates. Some of these will, unfortunately, be unspoken. If there are assumptions about your organisation that may inhibit the change you want to make, then make them explicit. By doing so you open up the possibility of their being challenged, and even if they remain, working to an assumption is at least a conscious decision.

Hence, continuing the examples used through this chapter, we can generate Table 2.6.

	Change objective	Examples of possible change constraints
1	To reduce our dependence on government funding	All alternative funding bodies will have to be approved by our funding agency and our ethics committee We must achieve the target level of funding from the private sector in 3 years
2	To increase the level of customer service we achieve	We can take up to 1 year to reach our target, but we must see some real improvement prior to that We cannot achieve our goal by lowering prices and margins on our products
3	To reduce the amount of office space we lease	We need to make the reduction by the end of the next financial year One of our leases is due for renewal in 6 months, which would be an opportunity We will not be reducing the number of staff we employ We cannot reduce the number of meeting rooms we have, although some can be made smaller We have to keep our existing main office We will not move overall geographic location to achieve this change We cannot make any significant investment
4	To develop the skills and competencies of our staff to be able to handle the future challenges and changes facing the business	Over time we will replace staff who leave voluntarily with staff with more appropriate skills, but we will not deliberately encourage any staff turnover to achieve our objective The change must be achieved with existing training budgets, but we can de-prioritise other training
5	To refresh our product set with new, innovative products	All new products must stay aligned with the current strategy of targeting consumers of an ABC1 demographical group via our existing retail partners The target must be reached within 2 years
6	To change our culture and environment to be a more enjoyable organisation to work in	We will not raise salaries, on average, by more than the rate of inflation – so the problem cannot be resolved by paying more We need to achieve the target by the end of this financial year
7	To improve the quality of orders processed	Any new order forms and processes must meet existing regulatory conditions and be easily adaptable as regulation changes We must achieve the objective within 6 months It must not jeopardise our achieving ISO 9000 accreditation It must not decrease our average order value or number of orders processed

Table 2.6 **Sample change constraints**

Step 2.8 **Define additional measures**

In step 2.4 (define your output measure and target) I described the need for an output measure to quantify your progress towards the result you are trying to achieve. However, you may need to measure at least three other types of activities:

- Input measures, quantifying the key factors that contribute to the output you want.
- Measures which enable you to understand the impact of your change upon the constraints you have identified.
- Measures related to the progress of the activities of the change initiative team (project measures).

The output measure enables you to understand if you are achieving the result you want. It does not, though, help you determine why you are currently achieving a certain level of result, or how you can achieve a better result. To understand this you must measure the things you do that achieve that result. Put another way, as well as measuring the result you achieve, you must measure the factors that contribute to this result; these are called 'input measures'.

As a simple example, imagine you want to lose weight. Your output measure is your weight in kilos. By measuring your weight regularly you will know at any point in time how well you are doing, and be able to understand the trend in your weight. Knowing that you weigh 83 kg today when you weighed 85 kg last week shows you are being successful, but it does not help you understand how this success is achieved. To give you this understanding, your input measures could include the number of calories of food a day you eat, and a record of how often you exercise. By tracking your output measure and input measures you can start to see how the amount you eat and the amount you exercise lead to the outcome of lower weight.

Why you achieve a particular result is determined by the way you tackle the causes of the gap between your result and your target. The input measures should be linked to the gaps you have identified. There may be many reasons for the gap and many input measures.

The next type of measure is related to your constraints. You want to avoid the situation where the whole organisation becomes focused on success and ignores your constraints. For example, you may want to increase profits. However, if it is important that you do not reduce customer satisfaction, then you need to measure this in parallel, to make sure it is not being adversely affected by your search for higher profits.

The final type of measure relates to the progress of your change initiative. You can consider the change initiative as a project, and, as with all projects, you should have ways for measuring progress, money spent, and so on.

These three types of measures are shown in Table 2.7.

Step 2.9 Identify sources of data

To use the measures chosen in steps 2.4 and 2.8 you need measurement data. For example, if your target is to decrease by 25% the floor space your organisation leases you must have data showing how much floor space you lease and data to measure the variation in floor space as your change proceeds. If your target is to achieve a 90% customer satisfaction rating, you need data showing what your customer satisfaction rating is. Data can be facts, numbers, results or statistics.

Good data will show you where you are at any time relative to your target, let you track progress, help to choose between options to achieve your change, and finally tell you when you have achieved your objective. An early part of your change programme is therefore to get some pertinent data.

If your measure of success is defined in terms of something you already measure then it is easy to find the data you need. Often, though, the data is not at hand, and you have to look for it. The first place to look is in your organisation's existing pool of management information. What is currently measured? What is currently collected? What is currently bought from other organisations? Sources of measurement information include data that comes out from existing processes and systems. You may be lucky and currently measure exactly what you need, or may be able to generate the data by correlating and combining data from existing sources. Also, data can be obtained from external sources, since there are lots of businesses which sell data on a commercial basis. Such can be useful for benchmarking or finding out about market trends, but it is rarely specific enough to support a change initiative.

Change objective/ output measure	Input measures	Measures of impact on constraints	Initiative progress measures
1 To reduce our dependence on government funding To have 25% of funding from private sector	Number of funding bodies identified Number of business relationships with key funding sources Number of funding applications made Percentage of applications successful	Percentage of applications rejected by the ethics committee	Time since start of initiative Percentage of target result achieved Percentage of planned time used Benefits achieved vs. time spent Cost since start of initiative Percentage of budgeted cost spent Benefits achieved vs. cost spent *(These measures are common to all the example change initiatives)*
2 To increase the level of customer service we achieve For at least 90% of our customers to rate us as good or very good for service	Number of complaints Fault rates PCA 30 (percentage of calls answered within 30 seconds) Top 5 dissatisfaction issues from customer surveys	Price, revenue and margins per product	
3 To reduce the amount of office space we lease To decrease the amount of office space we lease by 25%	Average area per member of staff Percentage of staff home-working Percentage of staff who could work from home Ratio of hot-desks to permanent desks Average utilisation of desks Average meeting room size Average meeting room utilisation Average meeting attendees and variance	Number of staff Number of meeting rooms	

▶

49

Change objective/ output measure	Input measures	Measures of impact on constraints	Initiative progress measures
4 To develop the skills and competencies of our staff to be able to handle the future challenges and changes facing the business To achieve 100% success rate in change initiatives we undertake	Percentage of staff applying for training Percentage of staff with change-management-based objectives Percentage of managers sponsoring and accountable for a change initiative	Training budget and percentage spent tracked across year	
5 To refresh our product set with new, innovative products To generate revenues of at least £5m from new products	Number of new product initiatives Total and average revenue from new products Number of new products launched per quarter Average time to deliver new products		
6 To change our culture and environment to be a more enjoyable organisation to work in For at least 75% of our staff to regard our organisation as an enjoyable place to work	Number of staff complaints Turnover of staff – percentage attrition Percentage of leavers stating company culture as a major issue Top 5 dissatisfaction issues from staff survey	Salary budget Percentage rise in salary per quarter	
7 To improve the quality of orders processed For 100% of order forms to be processed correctly, and for a maximum of 5% of orders to be rejected due to being incomplete or poorly filled in	Length of order form (number of fields) Average time to complete form Amount of repeat information on form Percentage of information that can be auto-filled and percentage that is Number of orders processed per day per member of staff	Average order value Number of orders processed per day Number of quality audit issues raised	

Table 2.7 Secondary measures

Sometimes really good data to direct your specific change does not currently exist in a readily available format. If it does not exist there is a temptation to proceed with a change without any supporting data, trusting to gut feeling and assumptions. You do have to be realistic because some data will never be available, or the cost to collect it will be too high. However, you must not assume this, and getting accurate and pertinent data is worth a lot of time, effort and investment. Without good data any decision you make is to some extent a guess, subject to risk and personal bias.

So what other sources of data are there? Consider finding data from:

- *Temporary measurements*: these are typically collected manually by staff during their normal activities. These can add significantly to effort, but are often worth it. As an example, a company processing insurance claims wants to know how complete the claims are. Therefore claims processing staff have been asked to maintain manual counters of well-completed and poorly completed forms every time they process a claim. This will add to the work of claims processing, but provides greater information which may be essential to get the change right.

- *New permanent measurements*: if the data you need is not only useful for your change programme, but helpful on an ongoing basis, why not take the opportunity now to design a process or system to collect data on an ongoing basis?

- *Interviews (staff and customers)*: you can perform your own research. Your staff will have a tremendous experience base, so talk to them! This is often an excellent source of information that is underutilised. Well-structured interviews can require significant effort, but will provide a good data source.

- *Consultancies*: activities such as benchmarking surveys can provide useful data. However, whilst benchmarking data often triggers change initiatives, usually it is often not specific, regular or detailed enough to drive a change programme, and may be prohibitively expensive to update regularly.

- *Academics*: universities and other academic institutions often have data about general trends. Although such data can help to identify change ideas, rarely is it specific enough to manage a change project.

In reality for many changes you must prepare for some manual collection of data. Putting processes in place to collect data, such as using check sheets with counts of actions and results from actions, takes time, and is often unpopular with the people who have to keep any counts as it adds to their work. It may not even be popular with some senior leaders in the organisation as it can be seen as simply a delay to taking action. Nevertheless, it is essential.

Whatever data you choose to collect there are a number of characteristics that differentiate good and bad data. There is a whole science on collecting and analysing data, which is well beyond the scope of this book, but some basic points always to remember are as follows:

- To understand what your data is measuring. Names used to describe data can be misleading. Check what the name of the data really means, what is the methodology used to collate and manipulate it, and what the sources are. Only accept the data if you understand it and are comfortable that the source and methodology are reasonable and reliable. For example, the concept of a customer satisfaction rating seems easy to understand, but unless you know how the data is collected, and what questions were asked of customers, it can be misleading. Asking customers how they feel about the service you provide, compared with asking how they feel about your prices, will give different pictures, and yet either could be part of a customer satisfaction survey.

- To take data from accurate and reliable sources that are auditable. If you are making important decisions based on any measurement data you need to have confidence in its reliability and accuracy. Auditing data not only ensures reliability and accuracy, but sends a clear signal to those who collect or create the data to ensure it meets your quality needs.

- To ensure data is up to date, and based on a measurement made within a timescale relevant to its use. If you want to understand current customer perceptions of your organisation it is no good using data that was collected a year ago.

- To understand how data has been manipulated, if it has. Statistical approaches have great power, but even very simple statistical tools can be misleading if you do not know them. Is an average a mean, a mode or a median? Do you really know what a standard deviation or a correlation measure tells you?

- For difficult to collect or very high volumes of data, use sampling if possible. Sampling is useful as it avoids your having to count every single instance of an event. However, for sampling to be appropriate the sample size must be statistically relevant and the process for sampling should be auditable to show there is no inherent bias in the way you sample.

- Single points of data are rarely reliable or useful. Good data has history so you can see trends, work out averages and see variations. Small samples are usually not statistically relevant. This means that any perception of an insight based on a small sample is more likely to be due to chance or coincidence than any underlying pattern. Reacting to and making decisions on individual pieces of data are usually no more valid than reacting or deciding upon no data at all.

- Good data is verifiable and not swayed by personal bias. Unless you do actually want to understand perceptions (such as for market research or staff satisfaction surveys), you want to avoid anecdotes, personal opinions and assumptions.

Sometimes there is no data available for what you want to measure. When this is the case organisations will often use a surrogate or indirect measure. For example, you may want to measure how good your staff are at running change projects, but this is quite difficult to assess in a reliable way. So, instead you measure how many of your staff have been on change management training courses as this is easy to track. Or perhaps you provide medical services and you want to measure how well you are treating patients. This is very hard to assess, so instead you use the more readily available measure of how long patients wait for an appointment. You may have no practical choice but to use such an alternative measure.

However, as previously shown in Table 2.3, whenever you drive success against a measure which is indirectly related or only a partial contributor to your objective, you will distort behaviour to some extent. People like to be successful, and they will try to be successful against whatever you measure success against. If you measure change management courses attended instead of success in running change projects you will find a lot of staff attending change management courses, but only partial improvement in actually managing change. Similarly, as a medical services organisation, if you measure patient waiting times instead of how well you treat patients you will find waiting times decreasing. Whether this is actually treating patients better is quite a different issue. This is the dilemma of measures, which can be the Midas touch driving performance excellence and the Achilles heel in organisations driving totally dysfunctional behaviour. If you have to use a surrogate or indirect measure you should at least be aware that it is not the perfect measure, and be alert for how it can distort behaviour.

Additionally, the task of collecting data is not free in any organisation. It takes time and effort, but unless the real measure of success is impossible or prohibitively expensive, it is worth the effort to find it, and invest in collecting the necessary data.

Continuing with our examples, Table 2.8 shows possible sources of measurement data for the output measure. You will, of course, need sources of data for your input measures as well. When you consider this you can see that the data collection for your change project may be a major undertaking. Don't baulk at it now – good data is worth a lot of effort!

	Change objectives	Target	Source of measurement data
1	To reduce our dependence on government funding	To have 25% of funding from sources other than the government (e.g. private sector)	Finance department's monthly funding reports
2	To increase the level of customer service we achieve	For at least 90% of our customers to rate us as good or very good for service in the monthly customer service survey	Monthly customer survey of minimum of 1,000 randomly selected customers
3	To reduce the amount of office space we lease	To decrease the amount of office space we require by 25%	Extract of information from facilities department on lease records. (Check with finance that these match what we are paying for)

Change objectives	Target	Source of measurement data
4 To develop the skills and competencies of our staff to be able to handle the future challenges and changes facing the business	100% success rate in change initiatives	We cannot measure this. Therefore we will use the following two surrogates: ● Percentage of staff who have attended the approved change management training course (target 100%) – HR will track ● Percentage of management staff who have had responsibility for running a change project (target 25%) – to be tracked through quarterly updates to personal development plans
5 To refresh our product set with new, innovative products	To generate revenues of at least £5m from new products	Finance department total monthly revenues by product line
6 To change our culture and environment to be a more enjoyable organisation to work in	For the quarterly staff satisfaction to show at least 75% of our staff regard us as enjoyable place to work	Quarterly staff satisfaction survey to all staff, to which we need responses from at least 50% of staff
7 To improve the quality of orders processed	For 100% of order forms to be processed correctly, and for a maximum of 5% of orders to be rejected due to being incomplete or poorly filled in	Manual count by order processing staff. Provide a control sheet for each member of staff to complete after each order processed with accept or fail, and if fail, reason codes for rejection

Table 2.8 **Sources of measurement data**

Step 2.10 Determine what you will change

By this point you have a lot of information to help you move forward with your change. You have a clear and measurable objective, and you have some clear and measurable opportunities for change. Now you must decide what route you are going to follow.

The decision you must make is to pursue one or more opportunities for change. If at this point you have only one opportunity for change (from step 2.6), then this step is not required, as you obviously must work on that opportunity. In most cases, though, you will have multiple choices and you must choose between them – and if you have identified only one opportunity you should be a little suspicious that you have not done enough work or are constraining your thinking with assumptions.

This stage is not about detailed planning, but about filtering and prioritising between options. You want to eliminate impractical options, and prioritise between options to match the gap you want to close and the level of resource you have available to work on the change. The time you take to perform this step, and the detail of the working, are dependent on the criticality of the change, the difference in benefits from pursuing different opportunities for change and the amount of resources you have. When you have a very critical change, limited resources, significant risk and major differences between options then the work must be robust and detailed. If you have plenty of resources, the change is not critical and many options can be followed, you really want to use this step for rapid high-level filtering and prioritisation.

What are you trying to achieve by choosing between opportunities for change? You are trying to select a limited number of actions to implement to meet your objective. There are six activities to complete before you can make your choice, each of which builds upon the information gathered in earlier steps:

- List all the different opportunities for change.
- Identify how much of the gap between your objective and your current status each opportunity will close.

- Estimate how much cost and resources each opportunity will consume to implement.
- Determine whether the opportunity is achievable.
- Determine whether the opportunity can be completed within your constraints.
- Take all of this information to filter and prioritise between opportunities.

I discuss each of these in turn.

Your first activity is to list the different opportunities for change. You identified these in step 2.6 (identify how to close the gap), and all you need to do now is to make sure they are documented. Some of the points you raised in step 2.6 may be phrased as causes of a gap (e.g. low product quality) and others were defined as an opportunity for change (e.g. reduce high product prices). Now is the time to become action focused, so all should be defined as opportunities for change, and hence rephrase the cause 'low product quality' to 'improve product quality'.

The second activity to determine what you will change is to identify how much of the gap between the objective and your current status each opportunity will close. This is one of the key reasons for collecting the data described earlier in this chapter, so you can make this decision as objectively as possible. Some opportunities for change will only have a small or marginal impact on the gap, and so unless these are very easy and quick to implement you probably want to ignore them. Some opportunities for change will have a very large impact on your gap, and these are the ones to prioritise.

The third activity is to estimate the amount of resources and cost each opportunity will require to be implemented. In terms of resources, you should not at this stage be trying to do a detailed assessment, but making a high-level estimate of how much money and resources are required. Accuracy is not critical at this stage, as you are not developing a business case or a plan, but trying to gain some objectivity in filtering and prioritising between options. You can use a simple subjective scale such as high, medium or low. Where you have a difficult choice between options you may need to do more detailed assessment.

The fourth and fifth activities relate to checking that the opportunity you have identified is achievable, and that it fits within your constraints. You want to discard any option that is not achievable in practice. For example, you may theoretically solve a problem by removing some government regulation, increasing competitors' prices or decreasing customers' aspirations, but these are not things your organisation can achieve. You also want to discard any opportunity that does not fit with your constraints. So, if you have a maximum of £100k to spend, an option that will cost £1m may be fantastic, but there is no point working on it.

A final point to introduce is the concept of quick wins. A quick win is a simple change management concept. As you deliver a change initiative it is beneficial to have some options to implement that will return a positive result quickly. A quick win may not deliver the significant improvement required, but it needs to be a visible and measurable improvement. The purpose of quick wins is twofold. Firstly, they ensure you achieve some benefit quickly, which is important in most organisations. Secondly, quick wins help to ensure that support for the change initiative grows. I will explain this concept in more detail in step 4.

All of these activities can be summarised in a simple tabular format. In Tables 2.9 and 2.10, I demonstrate by expanding two of the examples used in this chapter.

In the example in Table 2.9 I will reject opportunities 1 and 5 because they do not fit with the constraints this organisation is operating under (maximum of six months to deliver and no decrease in order volumes). I will start first with opportunities 3 and 4 because they consume limited resources and can be completed quickly. Then I will pursue opportunities 2 and 6 to make sure I reach the objective.

In the example in Table 2.10 I will reject opportunities 1, 3 and 6 because they do not meet my constraints as defined in Table 2.6. I will focus initially on opportunity 5 because it has a relatively low resource consumption and may be quickly implemented. Following this, if I have not achieved my objective I will implement opportunities 4 and 2.

Change objective	To improve the quality of orders processed
Target	For 100% of order forms to be processed correctly, and for a maximum of 5% of orders to be rejected due to being incomplete or poorly filled in
Gap to be closed	Currently unknown until we start measuring. However, anecdotally we think it is about 20% rejected, and a similar number incorrectly processed
Constraints	Any new order forms and processes must meet with existing regulatory conditions and be easily adaptable as regulation changes We must achieve the objective within 6 months It must not jeopardise our achieving ISO 9000 accreditation It must not decrease our average order value or number of orders processed

Opportunities for change	How much of gap can be closed with this opportunity?	How much resources will this consume?	Does this meet with your constraints?	Is the change achievable?	Quick win	Order to execute
1 Increase the amount of time the sales force has to complete order forms	50%	H	N	Y	N	n/a
2 Incentivise sales teams to get order forms right first time	50%	M	Y	Y	N	3=

▶

Opportunities for change	How much of gap can be closed with this opportunity?	How much resources will this consume?	Does this meet with your constraints?	Is the change achievable?	Quick win	Order to execute
3 Redesign order forms to be clear and unambiguous	25%	L	Y	Y	Y	1=
4 Redesign form to be less complex and remove duplicate information	25%	L	Y	Y	Y	1=
5 Apply new technology to automate process	100%+	H	N	Y	N	n/a
6 Improve skills in order processing teams	50%	M	Y	Y	N	3=

Table 2.9 Assessing opportunities for change – example 1

Change objective	To reduce the amount of office space we lease
Target	To decrease the amount of office space we require by 25%
Gap to be closed	We currently lease approximately 65,000 square feet of office space. We need to reduce the amount we lease by 1500 m²
Constraints	We need to make the reduction by the end of the next financial year One of our leases is for renewal in 6 months, which would be an opportunity We will not be reducing the number of staff we employ We cannot reduce the number of meeting rooms we have, although some can be made smaller We have to keep our existing main office We will not move overall geographic location to achieve this change We cannot make any significant investment

	Opportunities for change	How much of gap can be closed with this opportunity?	How much resources will this consume?	Does this meet with your constraints?	Is the change achievable?	Quick win	Order to execute
1	We have too many staff	100%	H	N	Y	N	n/a
2	We have too much space per member of staff	25%	M	Y	Y	N	3
3	We have too much ancillary space in the offices, e.g. meeting rooms and storage	25%	M	N	Y	N	n/a

▶

Opportunities for change	How much of gap can be closed with this opportunity?	How much resources will this consume?	Does this meet with your constraints?	Is the change achievable?	Quick win	Order to execute
4 People spend too much time in the office	25%	L	Y	Y	N	2
5 There is no hot-desking or home-working	50%	L	Y	Y	Y	1
6 We do not own our own property	100%	H	N	Y	N	n/a

Table 2.10 Assessing opportunities for change – example 2

Key tips

- To implement the most important changes you must be alert for change triggers.

- A clear objective is essential to drive a change programme. It acts as a compass for your work, and without one you are directionless.

- Good change is evidence based. It is measured against the pertinent and direct measure of success to achieve a predefined improvement using clear and accurate data to assess. Take advantage of great creative ideas and insights, but before you go further ensure the work you are about to undertake is really supported by evidence and data you understand from a reputable and auditable source.

- There are usually many different ways to achieve an objective. Good change initiatives review the different opportunities for change in a structured way, and select to take advantage of those opportunities which best achieve the objective within the constraints of your organisation.

- Good change decisions are open to challenge from those with different viewpoints and take account of the knowledge and experience of people at many different levels in the organisational hierarchy.

TO DO NOW

- Write down and review your current idea of your change objective – is it correct, clear, meaningful, unambiguous, concise, challenging and achievable?

- Identify any pertinent data relevant to your change that is already collected and available.

- Decide how you will approach gathering the rest of the data you need.

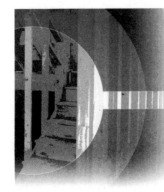

Step 3

Build the change team

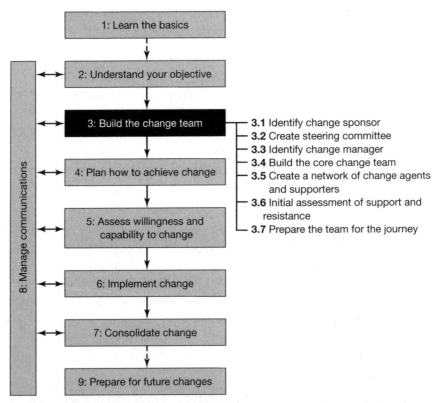

- 1: Learn the basics
- 2: Understand your objective
- 3: Build the change team
- 4: Plan how to achieve change
- 5: Assess willingness and capability to change
- 6: Implement change
- 7: Consolidate change
- 9: Prepare for future changes

8: Manage communications

- **3.1** Identify change sponsor
- **3.2** Create steering committee
- **3.3** Identify change manager
- **3.4** Build the core change team
- **3.5** Create a network of change agents and supporters
- **3.6** Initial assessment of support and resistance
- **3.7** Prepare the team for the journey

THIS CHAPTER COVERS:

- Building the team to deliver and implement your change.

THE CENTRAL POINT IS:

- Change will not just occur, it needs a set of motivated people performing a range of roles to make it happen. Although the full range of skilled resources required will vary from change to change, there are some common core roles always required.

Setting the scene

Consider the following three examples of change situations which show different aspects of the need for a change team:

1. A technology company's leadership team, made up of the executive directors, met for a biannual strategy planning session. As part of this session the group agreed the major activities and changes the business would make in the following year, and also reviewed the status of previously agreed initiatives. One investment the chief executive was particularly keen on was to build two new data centres in Europe. This was a major commitment and significant change in direction for this business, but when the directors met, the CEO outlined her case. The other directors soon understood her vision and acknowledged there was a very strong business case for building the data centres. So, it was agreed that the investment would be made. Six months later, at their next biannual strategy session, they started by reviewing progress on previously agreed initiatives. Soon it was time to discuss the data centre investment. The CEO raised the issue and asked how it was going. She was met with blank and slightly embarrassed looks. Each of the directors had agreed to support the idea – but no one had actually taken responsibility for driving it forward.

2. An IT manager was asked to submit a plan as part of the annual budget and corporate planning process for the next year within an organisation. This was to be the fourth year in succession that the IT manager had submitted his plan. In the previous three years the plans had been straightforward with some incremental investment on the preceding year, but essentially each year's plans had been similar to the year before. This year, the IT manager had spotted an opportunity for a radical change. It would require a significant investment, but the IT manager saw that the change he was proposing could give great benefits to the organisation. He worked diligently to produce a detailed case for his proposal, often working late at night and into the weekends. He was proud of this vision and wanted now to share it with the directors. His expectation was that they would be greatly impressed with his idea and this would reflect well on him. In fact, when he presented he was met with incomprehension and surprise. His boss simply stated that it was not what was expected and asked him to go back and present a more sensible plan and budget. Not only had he failed to get his idea across, but also he had actually created a negative image for himself.

3. A team had been working with the HR (human resources) function of an organisation to design and roll out a programme of management training. The organisation had realised that its managers did not have the skills for the challenges the organisation would face in the next few years. One partial solution to this was to design a series of 10 two-day training courses that together gave a common basic level of training to all managers in the organisation. Everyone thought this was a great idea. The team researched the training needs and developed a bespoke course that suited the organisation perfectly. Now was the time to roll out the courses. A communication was made to the business and managers were invited to apply for the courses. A month later and almost no-one had applied. Some research was done and the situation became clear. Although everyone thought the training was a good idea, no one felt they could actually afford the 20 days required to do the 10 modules. Most people seemed to have assumed that the training was for someone else! Many managers thought that if they personally took the time out for the training they would fail to meet their bosses' expectations and performance targets. The HR team had delivered a course but had not understood the real environment of the managers working in the business and how much time they could actually spend on training.

In all of these examples the change has failed, but the reason for failure is not the objective, which in each case was worthwhile and important. The problem in each example was the lack of a complete set of change responsibilities. In the first example, no one was actually tasked with doing the work, and so nobody did anything. Lack of resources allocated to any project will result in at least slow progress, and at worst no progress at all. In the second example, the work was done, but no one at a senior level was sponsoring or even aware of the work of the IT manager and so the directors were not prepared for it. When the IT manager presented, they probably did not even hear his great ideas as it was simply not what they were expecting. None of them helped the IT manager to get the support he required. Lack of senior management support or sponsorship is a very common cause of change being rejected. In the third example, the change team was cut off from the real operations of the organisation and had assumed that interest in the topic would automatically become commitment to doing the training. A lack of access to people who work in the operational areas, who can robustly test the change ideas, is another very common reason for change failure.

This chapter looks at what different skills and resources are needed in a change team to drive a change initiative to a successful conclusion.

Introduction to building the change team

The roles required to achieve a change successfully will vary from change to change. The material in this chapter therefore provides an overall set of roles required, to be tailored to the specific case of the change required. A very large and complex change typically requires a larger and broader set of skills than a small local modification in one department. However, generally the following are required:

- A change leader or sponsor
- A stakeholder group or steering committee
- A change manager
- A change team
- Change agents and interfaces with the different areas of the organisation affected by the change.

It is important to note that these are *roles* and *not people*. For smaller changes an individual may take many of these roles; for very large changes each role may be fulfilled by more than one individual.

Change does not occur spontaneously in organisations. For a change to take place in any organisation it is necessary for someone to identify the need for change, to explain this need to others in the organisation, and to gain support for making the change. This is the role of a *change leader* or *sponsor.*

Change sponsors are often senior executives, directors and top-level managers in an organisation. In a business context a change sponsor could be an executive who identifies that the competition is getting harder and so a business's cost base needs to be reduced, or its product line renewed. In a university it might be the vice-chancellor who sees that the way the university is funded must be modified with variations in student numbers. However, for small changes in an individual department the change leader may be the departmental head or team leader.

Great change sponsors are often charismatic and need to have good political skills to get others to see their view. They need to be confident and assertive in pushing the needs of the change. However, this does not mean that they do not listen to others. A change sponsor requires strong listening skills, as overcoming resistance often requires hearing and understanding others' viewpoints. Also, as change is often best understood from the viewpoint of people at lower levels in the organisational hierarchy (bottom-up change), a change sponsor needs the ability and the tendency to listen to more junior people.

A *change manager* is the person tasked with making a change happen successfully. The change manager is the person who manages and implements the change management approach – and is among the primary audiences for this book.

For minor changes and changes in smaller organisations the change sponsor may also be the change manager, but this is unlikely to be true for a complex change in a large organisation. Normally the change sponsor must appoint a change manager.

In one way the role of the change manager can be seen as analogous to the role of a project manager, and in many situations a change manager may also be a project manager. The change manager, like the project manager, is the person responsible for ensuring an objective is achieved by following a structured process. However, the skills, approach and focus of a change manager are different, and to some extent broader, whilst less structured and formalised from those normally employed by a project manager. Project managers are usually primarily focused on the deliverables from a project, whereas a change manager is primarily focused on implementation of those deliverables. For a manager to develop great delivery capabilities, he or she needs both project and change skills.

The *change team* is a group of people working under the direction of the change manager, who will complete the tasks necessary to deliver the change.

The *change steering committee* is a group of people who work with the change leader to direct and advise the change. The purpose of a change steering committee is to ensure that the diverse views of all those who may be affected by a change are considered, rather than purely those of the change leader. Change steering committees often comprise various senior managers in organisations, but the best committees include a range of influential participants, such as staff and even union representatives.

Change starts with one or more of these responsibilities. For example, if you are a change manager and you have no sponsor you must find one or face risk of failure. If you are a change sponsor without a change manager you must find one, allocate one from your own team or do it yourself!

This chapter describes these roles in more detail, but as changes vary hugely in scale, complexity and ambition, the information in this chapter has to be tailored by you to the needs of your specific situation.

How and when the change team is built

In most of this book the assumed audience is the change manager. The change manager sits at the heart of delivering change and is the person who will define the approach and steps to get the change delivered. However, this chapter is different as building a change team does not normally start with the change manager, but with the appointment of a change sponsor. It is the change sponsor who then selects and appoints the change steering committee and the change manager. The change manager then will go on to appoint the rest of the change team. However, in practice it can sometimes work in a different way. For example, I have seen the situation where a change manager was appointed by a permanently standing change steering committee. The change manager then requested the steering committee to allocate a change sponsor. The order does not really matter, as long as a full change team is created.

Whoever is responsible for building the change team must ensure that it provides the range of skills and quantity of resource to complete the change initiative. Simple checks include ensuring the change team:

- Has all the roles defined in this step.
- Provides the range of specialist skills needed (e.g. HR, legal, IT, business processes, communications, etc.).
- Is credible and has the political, influencing and communications capabilities required.
- Comes from a broad spectrum of the areas impacted by the change.
- Is a group of people who will work well together.
- Is made up of people who are available and who have time to perform the tasks required.

Potentially there is a problem with the order of the chapters in this book, between step 2 (understand your objective) and this step. Someone needs to do the work to understand the objective as defined in step 2, and this is normally the change manager or change sponsor. So part of the team actually has to be in place prior to step 2. However, you do not need your full change team until step 2 is completed. To avoid making the process overly complex I have consolidated all the team-building activities into one chapter. The reality is that you must apply judgement and common sense and build the change team up as your objectives become better understood. Steps 2 and 3 will sometimes need to occur in parallel, rather than always sequentially as the order of chapters indicates.

The step-by-step guide
STEP 3 – Build the change team

Step 3.1 Identify change sponsor

The change sponsor needs to be an individual who is senior enough in your organisation to be a credible leader of change; to allocate or influence the allocation of resources to your change; to be politically astute; and to be experienced and influential with senior peers. In addition the sponsor needs to be ideally a great communicator and listener, and passionate about the change you are making. If that seems a lot, it is! As it is difficult to find individuals regularly with all of these characteristics, most change sponsors are compromise choices to some degree. However, whilst by compromising on choice of change sponsor you do add risk to the change initiative, most managers can learn to be fully competent sponsors with appropriate coaching.

The level of seniority required in a change sponsor is a function of how large, and especially how broad, a change is. For a change in an individual department, the head of the department is normally senior enough. For a transformation across many divisions of a large organisation it will require someone at an executive or equivalent level. In this case, if the change sponsor is not the CEO (or equivalent), it must be someone who reports directly to the CEO.

The main responsibilities of the change sponsor include:

- Gaining initial approval from senior peers for the change to take place, and for any investment associated with the change.
- Setting up the necessary change steering committee (see step 3.2) and subsequently chairing it.
- Identifying and allocating a suitable change manager (see step 3.3).
- Directing the change manager, and ensuring that the change initiative maintains alignment with the change objective and the pace of change expected.
- Supporting the change manager in overcoming barriers, problems, and providing help with access to the right level of resources.

- Reviewing progress, reporting and generally supporting communication about the change initiatives. A senior change sponsor can often be involved in communications to a wide range of staff, but sponsors are particularly critical in communications to their peers and to the most senior levels of an organisation.

- Providing whatever support and action is appropriate and required to ensure the change initiative achieves its objectives.

The overall role can be summarised by saying that the change sponsor is accountable at a senior level for ensuring that the objective of the change is achieved.

The change sponsor is normally a senior executive who gives a proportion of time to the change initiative. This proportion will vary depending on the scale of change. Typically it is of the order of a few hours a week, although for the largest of business transformations it can be a full-time role reporting directly to the CEO.

Step 3.2 **Create steering committee**

Working with the change sponsor will be a steering committee made up of a representative sample of senior managers from the areas impacted by the change. The purpose of the steering committee is to:

- Support the change sponsor in gaining acceptance for the change and communicating progress.

- Make the necessary decisions associated with the change, especially when a decision requires cross-departmental consensus or has cross-departmental impact.

- Ensure that the variety of views about the change, from different parts of the organisation, is considered.

- Provide constructive challenge to proposed objectives, approaches to achieving them, and any assumptions about the change and its impact.

- Help the change sponsor drive any action required to make the change happen.

- Provide access to resources from across the company.

Much of the role relates to supporting the change sponsor and change manager. However, the steering committee is not simply a supporting team for the change sponsor, but should contain a true representative sample of viewpoints from the organisation. A group of 4 to 10 people is best. Any smaller and the steering group may not represent all the diversity of opinions in your organisation; any larger and, unless the sponsor is a really effective chairman or woman, it may be unproductive and unmanageable.

Although the steering committee members must work well together as a unit, it is important to avoid 'groupthink'. Groupthink is where a group of people working together start to meld so well as a team that they all think alike and do not challenge each other. One role of the steering committee is to provide support and access to resources, but critically it must also provide constructive challenge to the change sponsor. If everyone always agrees at the steering committee meetings then it may mean you are really lucky and working on one of those rare changes that everyone agrees with and there are no barriers to implementation, but it normally means you have the wrong group of people (or the right people working in the wrong way!).

Some committees will never get to a point of groupthink, but for others it happens too easily. Avoiding groupthink is achieved in a number of ways. It starts with the selection of the right steering committee members, who are chosen for a variety of viewpoints. It requires the sponsor actively to manage the committee to discuss the diversity of views, rather than seek the fastest way to resolve issues or the speediest way to end meetings. It also requires vigilance of committee members to challenge themselves about the assumptions and agreements they are making.

Although the steering committee is there to provide challenge, it must not undermine the change initiative. Hence, the rule for the steering committee must be to provide robust challenge to the change team and the change sponsor in committee meetings. It is equally important outside of steering committee meetings to show full support for the change irrespective of personal opinions. Additionally, although the steering committee will spend a high proportion of time in discussion and debate, its output must include real decisions and tangible actions.

The change steering committee is chaired by the change sponsor.

The term 'steering committee' can often create the image of a group which discusses and spends time arguing over meeting procedures without taking any action or making decisions. In some businesses the word 'committee' is treated with disdain. There is some confusion here between the concept of a group with different views which meets to make decisions, and a badly run group. There are many bad committees, but the concept of a committee is sound. The term 'committee' should not be treated as a negative one, but as an essential element for any change initiative. Of course, if the word 'committee' is completely unacceptable then another word – such as board, commission, executive, group or team – can be used, though the principles of operation and responsibilities are the same.

Step 3.3 Identify change manager

The change manager is the most critical role in any change initiative. This is the person who will run the change initiative on a day-to-day basis and has management responsibility for ensuring that it succeeds. The change manager is the person who drives the activity through the steps described in this book.

Change managers need to bring a variety of skills to the change initiative, including:

- The ability to select and motivate the change team.
- A structured approach to planning and managing tasks and activities.
- Action orientation and drive.
- Accountability orientation.
- Change management skills and experience.
- Good knowledge of the domain of the change (or an ability to learn it very quickly).
- Understanding of the organisation and culture.
- Good communication skills, in terms of transmitting information and equally importantly an ability to listen.
- The ability to balance empathy for any group with the capability to push action robustly to completion once a route has been agreed, even in the face of stiff opposition.

The role requires a well-experienced manager. Ideally the manager will have specific experience of delivering change before and had change management training. The level of commitment required of the change manager will depend on the scale of the change, but for a significant change this will be a full-time role. The best change managers understand the organisation and culture they are working in.

Sometimes interim managers and consultants are used as change managers, and this can work well if they have significant change expertise. However, to be successful the individual chosen must quickly understand and adapt to the specific environment of the organisation being changed. Without empathy and sensitivity for the organisation's culture, norms of behaviour and sensitivities, an external change manager may fail, or, worse, seem to succeed but create lasting damage by pushing through inappropriate change.

If you have no choice but to use an externally sourced change manager, such as consultants, it can help to pair them up with a permanent member of staff. Your line manager will bring knowledge of your organisation and your work, whilst the consultants will bring knowledge of change management practices and principles.

For the largest of changes there are two specific components of the change manager's role that may be separated out:

- *Project manager* – the project manager is responsible for the development of the plan for the change initiative (as described in step 4). This plan shows all the tasks necessary for completing the change, the order in which they must be done, and who does what. Having created the plan, the project manager is in essence responsible for monitoring and driving progress for the completion of the tasks.

- *Communication manager* – the communication manager is responsible for managing all the communication required on the change initiative. The specific communication needs for any change initiative vary considerably, but they are always an important component of successful change. This role and the tasks performed are described in more detail in step 8 (manage communications).

Step 3.4 **Build the core change team**

The change team is the set of people who work under the management of the change manager to make the change happen. The core change team is built up from a set of individuals who can allocate some or all of their working time to a change. For a very small change the change manager may be the change team(!); for large transformation programmes the change team may contain tens or even hundreds of people.

For a large transformation there are two types of people on your change team – the core team and supporting team. The core team contains those people who are permanently allocated to the change work and who are completely essential to doing what is required. Beyond this you may have a wider pool of people who at times provide specific support or complete specific tasks, but who are only required to do those tasks for a limited period in the life of the project. For example, change programmes often require some IT development. Where IT development is an essential component of the change then you will require one or more IT specialists in your core change team to ensure your requirements are collected and to manage this work. However, in most situations you would expect the actual IT development to be done in your IT department in the same way that it is done for anyone else in the organisation. You do not need the whole IT department to be brought in as part of the core change team, but only to provide supporting team members for the length of the development.

The specific make-up of a change team and the skills required depend on the type of change. It needs to be broad enough to avoid groupthink, but narrow enough to allow working together. It needs to contain the different skills and viewpoints required, and broadly understand the whole area impacted by the change. It needs sufficient power and influence to drive the change. The change team must be able to ensure as wide an involvement in the change from as many people as practical.

As most changes have an impact on people, the change team will commonly include some degree of HR involvement and, if your organisation has an internal communications department, support from that area as well. Many changes require people to learn new skills or to work according to different processes, so the learning and development or training department's involvement is often required. Very frequently change initiatives require enhancement and adaptations to IT systems and processes, so IT staff and business process specialists will be required. Beyond this, every change team is unique to the situation.

In step 4 we will look again at the resources needed in this team to work on your change once you have developed a change plan.

Step 3.5 Create a network of change agents and supporters

If the change you are undertaking is complex and cuts across many departments it is also very useful to identify a series of change agents across the organisation. A change agent is someone who supports the change you are undertaking, but also who understands in detail the operations, processes, systems and people in a specific area that the change will be implemented in. The various roles of change agents in their specific area of the business include:

- Enabling the change team really to understand the gap between the desired state and the current state. Often change initiatives start with a theoretical understanding of how an organisation operates. Many individuals will have strongly held beliefs about how processes should or could work; unfortunately these beliefs are often mistaken. The starting point for change is really to know how the organisation operates and to know how processes actually work. Only individuals with direct and current experience of the processes can provide this understanding.

- Providing a sounding board for the practicality and impact of the change in a specific area, by responding to change proposals and giving feedback on their viability. (Although members of the steering board also represent specific areas, their seniority may mean they do not know all the detailed implications of the change.)

- Gaining feedback and input from the area the change agent represents to change proposals. This network of change agents and supporters needs to feel involved in the design and implementation of the change. The more involved people are, the more likely they are to support the implementation. Hence this network should be made as wide as possible.

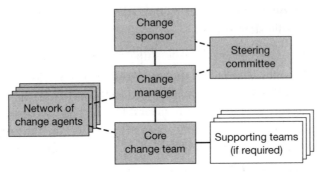

Figure 3.1 A simple change management organisation

- Acting as a supporter for change in a specific area on a day-to-day basis. This can be through answering staff questions about the change, and generally to communicating positive messages about the change on an ongoing basis.
- Attending meetings and workshops on the change and representing the needs of a specific area.

Building a network of change agents is not like building the rest of the change team. It will occur as the change progresses and when it is understood which areas of the organisation are impacted by the change and so where change agents are required.

Change agents may be relatively junior members of staff, but they need to be credible in their areas of the business, have a good network of contacts and relationships, know the area they represent, and have a positive disposition.

Figure 3.1 shows a simple picture of a whole change team. The solid lines show reporting lines in the context of the change project, and the dashed lines represent key relationships.

Step 3.6 Initial assessment of support and resistance

It is beneficial to start to develop an initial view of resistance and support for the change you are proposing. We will go into more detail on this in a later step, but clear thinking in this area is critical to good change implementation. There is no need to do a formal assessment at this stage, but you should consider the following:

- *Leadership team*: does the leadership of your organisation understand the change and do they fundamentally support its objectives? What could be the impact if they are not supportive? How will you leverage the supporters? If you really have no supporters in the leadership team the change is probably futile, unless it is not apparent to them. What could you do to get support?

- *Management team*: does the management of the organisation understand the change? Do they support the objectives and how they will be achieved? How can you leverage the supporting managers? Can those who are against be convinced by you or the sponsoring executive? If not, how will you handle them?

- *Staff*: what will be the impact of the change on staff in general? Will it be received positively or negatively? How will you manage this?

- *Other areas in the organisation*: are there groups or factions within each area, or are there any major sub-divisions or cliques that need to be considered?

- *Supporting stakeholders*: are there any other significant stakeholder groups, such as unions, customers or shareholders/funding bodies, whose views must be taken into account in this change?

Step 3.7 Prepare the team for the journey

There are many factors involved in building an effective team for your change project. A good team is made up of the right number of people, with the right skill sets. A good team is motivated and believes in the work it is setting out to do. A good team has a set of inter-personal dynamics between the team members that is productive and constructive. If you are in doubt always try to get the best resources you can, even if this means you end up with fewer people than you originally wanted.

The most effective teams are prepared for the work that they are about to undertake. The change sponsor and change manager should work together to ensure that all the team members are briefed. A good way to do this is to bring together all of those involved in the change for a briefing session. It is a bit of a cliché, but it is a cliché based on experience, that a change initiative is less about doing a predefined set of tasks and more akin to a journey to an unfamiliar destination. On starting you are not sure of all of the steps to get there, and to achieve this you must work openly and with trust. The briefing session is to set everyone's expectations and make sure they are starting out in the right direction.

The most important items to cover at such a briefing session are to:

- Describe the objective, measures, targets and opportunities for change you have identified.

- Make sure everyone knows their roles and level of input expected. This includes clarifying whether they are part time or full time, and what happens to their normal workload. Will it be handed off to someone else, will there be backfill, or are they simply expected to do this on top of their normal work? Unless the role is either short term or needs limited input, such as attending meetings, doing complex change work on top of all normal work should be avoided as it can jeopardise the project. (Backfill is when someone is temporarily employed in a role to cover for someone else doing a project-based task for a limited period of time. For example, if your organisation runs a production line, and your change project needs people from the production line to help you understand it, whilst these individuals are in the change team you may backfill them with contract staff to work on the production line.)

- Set expectations as to what it is going to be like to work on this change. It will probably be more chaotic than you would ideally like, but that is the nature of change programmes at times, and everyone must be prepared for this. It may be challenging in terms of the hours worked and the level of sheer intellectual effort. Occasionally, change can be emotionally draining.

- Stress the characteristics of people that will make this work. In truth this is good practice in any role, but particularly important in change. Change is about team work, not individual brilliance or heroics. Change is about working with people, so communication skills are of paramount importance, particularly taking time to listen. Change is helped by, and sometimes absolutely requires, passion, drive and belief in the end objective.

- Outline your findings from step 3.6 (initial assessment of support and resistance). Will people generally be in favour of or against this change? How should the change team members respond to any unsupportive challenge?

- Deal with change team members' concerns. People will have some concerns throughout a change project, but many can be put to rest now. A team with fewer concerns is likely to be more productive. It's not possible to plan for all the questions people may have, but typical concerns for people on change teams will include:

  - What happens to their normal work whilst on the change team?

  - For staff who are eligible for overtime, will this still be paid? (Sometimes this question is driven by people worrying about too much work, but it may be people actually worrying about earning less.)

  - Will there be a job to go back to when they have finished?

  - Where will they work? From their normal location, or will a special area be set aside for the change team? Will this mean additional travel or nights away from home?

  - How will their performance be assessed?

  - Will they have to make people redundant? What support will they have in doing this?

  - Why were they personally chosen?

Key tips

- There are two key roles in change management: the change leader, responsible for identifying the need for change and sponsoring the work to make a change at a senior level; and the change manager, responsible for making the change happen.

- There are two key supporting groups in change management. The change team, which works with the change manager to make the change happen, and the change steering committee, which ensures that a multiplicity of views are considered and that roadblocks are removed.

● The likelihood of success of a change will be increased by having a network of people in different areas of an organisation who can be used as sounding boards to check change concepts, to gain feedback on change proposals from those areas, and to support the change when it is implemented.

TO DO NOW

- ● Identify who you ideally want on your change team.

- ● Confirm that this team will provide you with the range of skills required:

  - ● Does this group provide the specialist skills you need (e.g. HR, legal, IT, business processes, communications, etc.)?

  - ● Will this group be credible and have the political, influencing and communications capabilities required?

  - ● Does the team come from a broad spectrum of the areas impacted by the change? If not, how will you understand the impact in those areas and work to get their buy-in?

  - ● Will this team of people work well together?

  - ● Are they available and do they have time to perform the tasks you require?

- ● Confirm that you have the necessary level of actively involved and supportive sponsorship.

Step 4

Plan how to achieve change

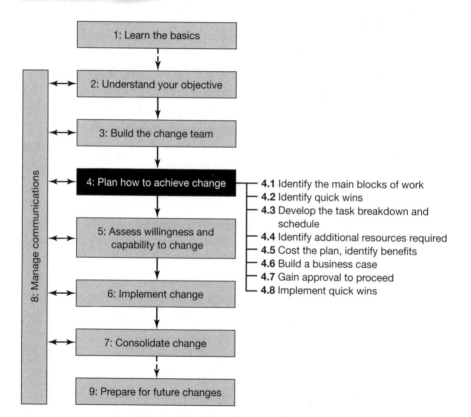

1: Learn the basics

2: Understand your objective

3: Build the change team

4: Plan how to achieve change
- **4.1** Identify the main blocks of work
- **4.2** Identify quick wins
- **4.3** Develop the task breakdown and schedule
- **4.4** Identify additional resources required
- **4.5** Cost the plan, identify benefits
- **4.6** Build a business case
- **4.7** Gain approval to proceed
- **4.8** Implement quick wins

5: Assess willingness and capability to change

6: Implement change

7: Consolidate change

9: Prepare for future changes

8: Manage communications

THIS CHAPTER COVERS:

- Developing a budgeted and approved plan of action to implement your change.

THE CENTRAL POINT IS:

- Change is a complex activity, and it should be controlled with a comprehensive, well-ordered and flexible plan.

Setting the scene

As an introduction to planning for change, consider the following four examples showing problems related to insufficient or ineffective planning:

1. The manager responsible for order processing was asked by his head of department to make improvements in the way customer orders were handled. Orders were taking too long to process and too many were being rejected. The manager was keen to improve on this situation and energetic to get it done. As soon as he had completed the discussion with his boss, his mind was whirring with creative ideas. Within minutes he was on the phone and firing off emails. He immediately tasked people with actions to improve the situation. Over the next few weeks he was constantly running around and making tweaks to processes, procedures and order forms, as well as tampering with system parameters. If energy was the measure of success then he was most successful, as he was obviously the most energetic manager around. Unfortunately, after a few weeks the level of performance in order processing was actually lower than before, staff felt lost in a welter of minor modifications which they had trouble keeping track of, and worse still the manager had run out of ideas as to what to change next.

2. The head of customer services wanted to improve the work of her department. She was a very detailed, structured and logical thinker. She understood her objective and the required change fully, and decided that before moving into implementation she would develop a detailed implementation plan. She started by breaking the objective into a series of smaller tasks. She did not understand all of the tasks fully or how people would respond to the changes, but made some guesses about how long each task would take, and what smaller activities they would break into. She analysed each of the

smaller activities and broke them down further still. She continued to do this until she had a very detailed plan with several hundred tasks, some less than a day long. By breaking down the plan into this detail she felt she really understood what needed to be done, and could completely control it. The change project was started, but did not work out according to her plan. Within a month there were literally hundreds of updates required to the plan. The head of department found herself spending more time maintaining the plan in line with what was really happening than taking part in any active management of the change.

3. A consultant was brought into a public sector organisation to help drive a change initiative. The finance department had to modify processes because of the way the government was funding this department, and also wanted to alter how budgets and spend were reported. The consultant was chosen because she had successfully done a similar piece of work at another government department a few months earlier. On arrival the consultant's depth of knowledge and speed to develop a detailed plan were impressive. The problem was that she had not developed a new plan, but was using the plan from her previous client. Very quickly the plan proved itself to be wrong in some key areas. On the surface this department was similar to the previous one she had worked at, but at a detailed level many things were different.

4. An experienced manager was brought in to run a large and highly complex change initiative. This change required the replacement of several core IT systems, new processes to be designed and implemented, over 250 new people recruited into the organisation, significant training work, and the closure of two offices in different parts of the country with the loss of 450 roles. The manager developed a well-balanced plan that was really tailored to this situation. After nine months the project was going well, from the manager's viewpoint, as the project was both in line with the time in the original plan and below budget. He expected to start completing the project in another six months. He was surprised when he was called in to see one of the members of the steering committee who harangued him, and repeatedly told him that the committee could not wait for much longer to start to see results.

In all of these examples the problems with the change activity could have been overcome by better planning. In the first example, there simply was not a plan, and this tends to result in random wasted effort. We do not need plans for most of the things we do in daily life because they are not that complex. But for any complex activity a plan has many benefits. It is only by starting with a plan that you can understand how long a task will take and how many resources it will require. The activity of creating a plan forces you to think before acting. A clear plan provides a document that you can explain your change with. Also, most importantly, the plan provides a way to manage work through the period of change.

In the second example we have the opposite extreme: there is a plan – in fact there is too much of a plan. Change initiatives are not like sticking a series of Lego blocks together at a predetermined speed. There are too many unknowns, too many variables that can change. A change plan has to be flexible, and more flexible than many project managers are often comfortable with. At the start of a change initiative the path to reach your objective is often not fully understood and the size and scale of many of the tasks will not be as you expect. The answer to this is not to avoid planning, neither is it to try and over analyse every task based on dubious assumptions and guesses, but to plan and to be willing to adapt your plan as reality exposes itself. All project plans need to be flexible, but those associated with change initiatives need to be particularly so. This means that the level of granularity in the plan has to be appropriate. Breaking tasks into blocks of activity a few hours long is normally futile. Many activities on change plans will be shown in blocks of a week or more. Sometimes parts of the plan can only be made up of key milestones for the major events that will occur, and progress can only be tracked relative to those milestones.

In the third example there should be a good basis for success, by having a very experienced consultant with relevant knowledge to manage the change. Unfortunately, rather than applying her knowledge to this specific situation, the consultant is lazy (or not as bright as she appears) and thinks she can simply use a template plan from another client. Very soon all that has happened is that she has lost credibility, and, if this organisation has any sense, her contract. By all means start by looking at old plans of similar projects for ideas and a view of structure for the plan, but each and every plan has to be unique to the situation.

The final scenario is a familiar trap for those experienced with any big project. Complex activities can take a long time to complete, but many members of an organisation will be impatient to see results. Worse, if they do not see any results they will lose patience with a change initiative and may even stop it. So, how can you manage to avoid this and yet still deliver complex activity that takes time to complete? There are two main answers. The first is to identify quick wins, small things with a real benefit you can complete rapidly when the change project starts. These will give the organisation some gains, as well as ensuring that people retain their belief in the project by seeing real improvements. The other way is to break a long plan into phases, and try to give some benefits at the end of each phase. It may take a year or more to complete a complex IT development, but that does not mean that some new parts of the system cannot be implemented in three, six or nine months.

Introduction to planning how to achieve change

Well-run change initiatives are managed with a considered and documented plan. Planning is a project management discipline, and by using even simple planning techniques you are considering your change initiative as a project. Although you can argue that all projects are changes, and all changes are projects, the sort of changes being discussed in this book – organisational changes – are very specific types of project. Not all project management techniques add value in these situations, but planning is a good starting point for even the most un-project-like of changes.

A full explanation of how to develop a plan is best left to project management books. However, it is valuable to understand the basics, and often these basics are enough. If your change is really complex it is worth having some professional project management support for developing the plans.

The aim of planning is to develop a document which describes the tasks you need to do, the order they must be done in, and who does what task. The plan enables you to:

● Understand how long a change initiative will take, and how much it will cost to do.

- Explain the change initiative to other people.
- Allocate work to different people in the change team.
- Manage your change initiative to successful completion.

All project plans need some degree of flexibility in them, but for change projects flexibility is particularly important. The plan is a guide to your intentions and expectations, though reality may work out differently. At the start of a change project you do not know for certain everything that needs to be done, how long each task will actually take, or how people will react to change. However long you spend on analysis and assessment, there will be some degree of error in your plan, and it is no good trying to stick to what is an invalid plan. This may lead you to conclude that you are better off without a plan altogether, or that planning is a waste of time. This is the wrong conclusion. Even if a plan is not quite right it gives you a structure to work with, and a framework which you can adapt. The problem of working totally without a plan is that it will often lead to complete chaos and you will not even have targets to aim at. With a plan you have a direction to go in, even if you need to amend it in response to what really happens. A change project is like a journey into unknown territory, and as such it needs to be able to adapt flexibly to whatever unexpected terrain the territory holds, but you still want to start with a clear understanding of the bearing you are following. Your plan provides this.

Change plans are often best thought of as a series of milestones you want to achieve as much as a complete description of all the activities required. One way of looking at changes is whether they are hard or soft. This is a crude but helpful categorisation. A hard change has a clear end point and well-understood tasks to undertake to deliver it. A good example of a hard change is an IT systems development. A soft change is a more nebulous idea that does not have an absolutely definite end point, and the tasks to get to that end point will evolve as the work progresses. A good example of a soft change is cultural change. Hard changes are usually possible to plan in detail; very soft changes are more difficult to plan. It is often possible with soft changes to plan the steps you initially want to undertake, but you will not be certain of the outcome until you have done them, and therefore you want to be able to adapt the plan as you go along and rely more on achieving milestones than very detailed task lists.

Every change is unique. Even if what you are trying to do has been done many times before, because the combination of the nature of the organisation you are working in, the particular set of people you are working with, and the way they will respond to change is unique, so the supporting plan must be unique too. It is no good having a plan which does not relate to what you need to do in your specific situation. By all means look at the plans from those projects as they can give you valuable insight and ideas on the actions you need to take, how long they typically take, and what sort of resources you need, but you must tailor them to your specific situation.

The level of detail in a change plan depends on the situation. My rule of thumb for managing any project is to try to get to chunks of work that are no shorter than a day, and not much longer than a week. This is a guideline, not set in stone – some important tasks may only take a couple of hours, but have to be shown on the plan. Some activities take a month or two and cannot be broken down. But these are exceptions. Have too many small tasks in your plan and you will get lost in the detail; have too many larger tasks and you will have difficulty managing progress. With a change initiative you may not be able to go into the same level of detail throughout all stages of the plan as you might expect on some projects. Let's look at a situation in which you are trying to achieve a cultural change. Some of the required actions, such as staff communication and training events, can be planned in detail. But much of the success will require thousands of cumulative changes in behaviour, and the actual achievement of cultural change is something that happens over time and cannot be meaningfully broken down into detailed discrete tasks in a plan. The level of detail, or granularity, in the plan must be appropriate to what you are trying to do.

A key concept in change management is the idea of quick wins. Quick wins are exactly what they are called – things that are easy to do as part of your change initiative that can be done in a short period of time, and are a win or benefit for your organisation. Quick wins are normally implemented at the start of a change initiative. There are two main advantages to having quick wins, and many change management practitioners consider them as mandatory. The first advantage is that you rapidly achieve some benefit for your organisation, and the sooner you achieve a benefit, the more benefit that will accrue over time. The second, and in many ways more important, advantage from a change management perspective is that by giving improvements you will win people over and start to develop belief in your project. Quick wins help to generate support and overcome any resistance people have to a specific initiative.

Another useful planning concept is that of phasing. Instead of planning your whole project in the same level of detail, and instead of working to one single end date when you deliver everything, you break the project into phases. The first phase is the most detailed. In some situations you only actually commit to completing the first phase in the planned time. Phasing helps to avoid worrying about detailed planning for far-off events that you don't yet understand. It also means that your organisation does not have to wait until the end of the whole initiative to gain all the benefits. Consider a house builder who has a project to build 100 houses. The builder could design, plan and build all 100 houses and then sell them, but this means he will not make any return until he has built all 100 houses. It may be better to build the houses in four phases of 25 houses, selling each set of 25 as soon as they are built. This way the builder can start to see some sales in a shorter period of time.

In large change initiatives phasing is often crucial. The organisation is often hungry for benefits and by breaking up the change into phases you can feed this hunger. Also, large changes can have significant risk associated with them; by breaking up the change into smaller chunks the risk can be reduced. When an organisation wants to redesign core processes you could choose to work on redesigning all processes in parallel. However, by phasing, you work on one process at a time, the risk of disruption to the organisation is reduced, and the time to complete the work on one process can be relatively short.

The step-by-step guide
STEP 4 – Plan how to achieve change

Step 4.1 Identify the main blocks of work

By now you should understand quite a lot about your change. You know your objective and what needs to change to meet this objective. You have a team to pursue that objective. You are in a good position to develop your change plan which will give you a clear, ordered and sized set of tasks to implement your change.

Knowing what you want to achieve, the next question you need to ask yourself is: 'What are the core components of work that must be done to achieve this change?' Understanding the core components, or blocks, of work is the first step to developing a plan. You are not yet trying to work out how hard or how big these pieces of work are, simply what they are. To put this in perspective, an example of the blocks of work that may need to be done in a typical change initiative for a sales function could be:

- Defining new sales policy and rules.
- Developing a new set of processes and procedures to meet that policy.
- Designing and implementing a new IT system to automate as much of the process as possible.
- Identifying who will be affected by the change in the sales, order processing and sales administration functions.
- Reviewing and enhancing organisational responsibilities and boundaries to align with the new processes, which should mean that the sales staff can do more things themselves and some support and administrative staff will no longer be required and will lose their jobs.
- Running some communication events to explain the changes and set people's expectations.
- Finding a way to motivate staff who will lose their jobs as part of the change to keep working until the change is complete.
- Designing training and holding training sessions so staff can learn how to work to the new processes and IT systems.
- Setting up a support and help desk for staff to ask questions about the changes during the life of the project.
- Dealing with redundancy or redeployment for the staff who will lose their jobs.

Your aim right now is not to go into any detail, but to try to get comprehensive cover of all the different aspects of work that need to be done to make your change happen. Also, don't worry about the order of tasks, but try to ensure that you have documented all the main chunks of work that need to be done. If you are unsure about something, include it for now.

To ensure you develop a comprehensive list of the main blocks of work, it is best to involve other people in this activity. Unless you really have tremendous experience it is likely that for any significant change activity you will overlook something. The best people to work with on this are your core change team, especially anyone who has experience of similar work.

If you have access to plans from other similar change initiatives, look at them. Remember the warning in the introduction: plans need to be specific to your situation; old plans can still be useful to look through and see if they have any blocks of work that are relevant to what you are doing and have not yet included. It is also worth now skimming through the contents of steps 6, 7 and 8, to check for major activities there that have to be built into your plan.

A simple way to identify the chunks of work is to do the following three activities:

- Work by yourself and document a provisional list of the major pieces of work. The aim is not to achieve completeness, but a starting point that can be discussed as a team.

- Bring your core change team together for a review meeting. (If your core change team is very large choose about 6–10 people with good and varied change experience for this session.) The task is to identify gaps, omissions and unnecessary blocks. The review will only take 30 minutes to an hour.

- Consolidate your original list with the output from the meeting. You should now have a good idea of the main pieces of work for your change initiative.

It is efficient to use the same meeting to have a brainstorming session to identify quick wins as well.

In documenting the list of main parts of the work, don't forget about data. Earlier in this book I discussed the need to identify the data required to measure and manage your change. You will need to continue to collect pertinent management data as part of your project. Therefore, if it is relevant, make sure that at least one of your main chunks of work is related to collecting and analysing data.

As well as data for your change initiative, you will often want to ensure that you have data for ongoing management once the change initiative is complete. (Such data is normally called management information or MI.) If you are going to deliver better management information as part of your project, now is the time to start considering it. All too often it is left to the later stages of a project, which means it is not done properly. As you are defining your major pieces of work for your change initiative ask yourself and your team if there should be a chunk of work about developing longer term management information.

Step 4.2 Identify quick wins

The next step is to identify any quick wins that you will deliver in this change initiative. If your project is very small and liable to take only a few weeks to complete, you can usually ignore quick wins.

Let's look at the words 'quick' and 'win' in this context:

- *What counts as a 'win'?* In the context of a change initiative a win is an improvement that is visible, has some tangible benefit, and is popular with those impacted by the project. The win does not have to be terribly profound or have a long-term lasting impact on your organisation, but it does need to be something that you can talk about and people will agree it is a good thing. The best quick wins are easy and cheap to implement and create a lot of positive discussion about the change initiative.

- *What is 'quick'?* Quick is relative to the scale of your change initiative. In my experience anything that takes longer than three months is not really quick, but anything less than that can be considered. For a change initiative that is only going to be a few weeks long then quick wins are probably irrelevant. On the other hand, if your change initiative really is only a few weeks long, you may be able to use the initiative as a quick win for a larger change programme. Quick wins may be achieved in a few days, though if they are they are often trivial. However, do not underestimate how much better you can make people's lives with some very simple alterations in processes, forms, systems, etc. Normally they take a few weeks of effort and investment.

Some examples of quick wins are:

- In an initiative to reduce order processing errors remove some unnecessary information from a paper-based order form. Often information is duplicated on forms. If you remove duplications you increase the speed to process orders and reduce the chance for errors.

- In an initiative to improve staff satisfaction within an office, start by providing coffee and tea-making facilities for staff without them. This could save staff time and money, costs little and is easy to implement.

- As a quick win in a business process redesign project co-locate key individuals from teams that are having trouble working constructively together. By bringing people close together they will start to understand each other's issues and styles of working of the other team. This is a great way to start off a change initiative aimed at improving interactions across departmental boundaries.

- In a business wanting to improve levels of service to its customers, provide engineers with stickers of contact numbers to place on equipment installed in customer's homes. Then the customer knows quickly who to contact for support and will not have to go searching for the right number. It also avoids the problems of customers ringing any other number in the organisation.

- As a quick win in a project to develop a new management information system develop some simple management reports using a spreadsheet. This can allow managers to focus on key points of a process, before a longer term IT solution is developed.

Quick wins should be relevant to the project. I once ran a project where the project team identified a quick win as putting in some new bicycle racks in an office to which quite a few staff would cycle if only they had somewhere to leave their bicycles. It was easy and cheap to do, was visible, benefited both the organisation overall and many staff individually, and consequently was popular. However, it had nothing to do with the core project, which was about speeding up product development, and therefore did not really generate any goodwill towards it!

There are many ways to identify quick wins, such as:

- **Brainstorming with your core team and network of supporters:** run one or, for big initiatives, a series of brainstorming sessions about what to change. From this you will generate lots of ideas for quick wins as well as ideas for the overall change initiative.

- *Observing and listening*: observe people at work and listen to their conversations. What causes problems or issues? Is there anything that you can see that could be easily, quickly and cheaply changed? Walk the floor, see people at work and you will often see many things that can be improved.

- *Asking*: in the area where you are making change ask the teams what makes their lives difficult. If they could change one or a few things, what would they be? If they could change any one small thing, what would it be? Some of the ideas will be impractical, some will actually be quite big, and you may therefore want to consider them as part of the main change initiative, but often people will come up with really creative and simple ideas that make their lives better and have a tangible benefit for your organisation.

- *Being open to offers*: have an open policy where anyone in the areas impacted by your change can talk to you, call you or send you an email with suggestions.

If you take people's ideas there is one thing you must do, and that is respond to each one. Even if ideas are crazy or impractical you should thank people for the suggestion, and tell them if you are going to implement it or not. If you do not implement the idea try to tell people why. Doing this keeps people interested. If you simply take people's ideas and don't give them credit you will irritate them. If you listen and then ignore what you have been told you will quickly gain a group of people who are antagonistic to the change initiative.

A further word of caution: before you implement a quick win, do be sure you understand the impact. Occasionally I have seen quick wins that seemed simple and very beneficial creating problems elsewhere in an organisation. Once I arranged for some parts to be removed from a form that staff had to complete as no one seemed to use the information and it took a long time to collate. Within a few days of implementing this small change I received a very angry call from another part of the organisation that could not do its work as the information it required was now missing!

Your quick wins will form part of your plan of work, and once you have your work approved you will implement them. However, if you have any quick wins that really do not need approval, that have an impact that is fully understood, that are easy and consume very little resource to implement, then go ahead and implement them now.

In this section I have focused on wins at the start of your change initiative, and these are very important. However, ideally you should identify not only a set of quick wins for the beginning of the change project, but a stream of regular wins across the life of the change. If your change is implemented as a series of phases this should deliver a regular stream of benefits to your organisation. Whenever there are prolonged gaps between benefits being delivered then you should always look to deliver smaller wins to maintain enthusiasm and momentum for the change.

Step 4.3 Develop the task breakdown and schedule

With an understanding of the major chunks of work and a list of quick wins you are ready to produce your plan. A good plan is simple, easy to communicate, achievable and measurable. There are eleven main activities to building a project plan:

1. Starting with the main blocks of work you identified (in step 4.1), divide the overall change initiative into its component tasks. Continually divide the main chunks of work into smaller tasks until you have a comprehensive list of things that must be done to complete the project. Don't forget to add your quick wins to the plan.

2. Estimate the length of time each task will take. If many of your tasks are less than a day long then you have probably gone into too much detail. If most of them are longer than a month you probably have not gone into enough detail really to manage the project.

3. Identify any dependency between tasks. A dependency is a link between tasks that forces an order upon tasks. For example, if your change requires you to make people redundant, you must inform them first, consult with them, and then make them redundant. You cannot do these tasks in any other order as there is a dependency between them.

4. Order the tasks into the right sequence using the dependencies you have identified.

5. Determine the people, money and other resources you need to meet this plan, and determine their associated costs.

6. Check what resources you actually have available, and refine your plan to take account of this. Once you have done this you have a complete first-cut plan.

7. If your plan is any longer than three months review whether you can break it up into phases. If it is longer than one year you should definitely phase the project. The underlying question to ask is: can you break the work down so you will deliver some or any benefit earlier?

8. Review the constraints you identified in step 2.7 (define your change constraints). Is the plan consistent with them? For example, if you have a constraint that your change must be achieved in six months and your plan shows it being done in four months, it is consistent, but if your plan shows the work will take eight months it is not consistent. If your plan is not consistent with the identified constraints, can you do it in a different way so that it is?

9. Review the plan: does it really match your needs? Looking at the plan, can you actually do it, and should you do it? Is there any better way it can be done? Normally a plan is just one way of achieving an objective, and there are other ways of ordering and scheduling the tasks.

10. Add some contingency to the plan: contingency is a buffer to account for risks and unforeseen events. Unless you have done very similar changes many times before, you will not know exactly how long every task will take, or even what every task is. Depending on how well you understand the tasks, and how much risk there is in doing those tasks, you will need more or less contingency. For a well-understood and defined task sufficient contingency may be about 10%; for a poorly understood and high-risk activity it should be much more.

11. One thing to make sure you include in your plan is any approvals you need to move your change initiative forward. This is discussed in step 4.7 below, but is often forgotten when developing a plan. Waiting on decisions to approve a change initiative is a common reason for delay in change projects, yet in reality there should be no excuse for experienced managers forgetting to include the time it takes to get approvals into their plans. Any significant investment

usually needs approval in most organisations, and this approval normally takes some time.

Good planning is crucial to any well-run project. If you are struggling, seek advice from a professional project manager.

Step 4.4 Identify additional resources required

In step 3 you built your core change team. Now that you have developed a plan you are in a position to see if you need any other resources to fulfil your change. Every activity on your change plan needs to be allocated to someone with the right skills and the time available to do that task. When you look through your plan you will often find tasks that cannot be done by your core team.

In some instances you will need to expand your core team. In many others you will only need access to people for short periods of time on the project. For example, if your change will result in new contracts, you will almost certainly need some legal support, but you may not require a full-time legal representative on the project. Alternatively, you may have a major piece of software to develop, but you will ask the IT department in your organisation to do this as part of its normal project workload. Although you will oversee the development, you probably don't want all the IT staff in your project team. In this case you would consider the IT department as one of the supporting teams.

When you have identified the additional resources you need, you must make sure they know when they will be required to work on the change initiative and what they will be required to do.

Step 4.5 Cost the plan, identify benefits

It is imperative to understand how much it is going to cost to implement a change, but the precise way you go about this will be specific to your organisation. The need for a full and detailed cost breakdown will vary from organisation to organisation. Some organisations have extremely tight cost control and even relatively small expenditures of a few thousand pounds have to be analysed in detail and justified. In others, quite junior managers can spend tens of thousands of pounds without recourse to a more senior manager's authority, and without too much scrutiny. Different types of costs receive different accounting treatments depending on the organisation you work in. There will always be a split between capital and operating expenditures, but you will have your own capitalisation policies, and so on. I have ignored this complexity, but you will have to make yourself aware of the financial processes and controls in your own organisation.

To understand the costs of a specific change, you need to consider two types of expenditure your organisation will be exposed to:

- *Implementation costs*: these are costs which are associated with doing the tasks in the plan you defined earlier in step 4.3. They will be the costs of doing every activity, including the cost of people's time and anything you need to buy to carry out the project.

- *Operational costs*: these are any new or additional costs your organisation will be exposed to once your change is complete. So, if as part of your change you will hire an extra 10 people, then the wages and associated costs for these 10 people are operational costs. If you develop new software as part of your change, the development costs may be considered by you as implementation costs, but software normally has maintenance fees associated with it and this is also an operational cost.

Often you can apply different accounting treatments to implementation costs and operational costs which can greatly affect the viability of the change, so it is important to understand the difference.

Before finalising your costs make sure you have considered any hidden costs that result from the change initiative. If you make a change in one part of an organisation it will often have an impact on another area. If costs rise elsewhere as a result of a change, then those costs should be considered as part of the cost of implementing your plan.

Next, identify any benefits that your change will bring about, and, if you can, the value of these in financial terms. Defining benefits in financial terms is important because it gives a common basis for comparison. If I say an organisation can spend £1m to improve customer satisfaction by

10%, it is not possible really to know if this is a good investment or not. However, if I can say that a 10% increase in customer satisfaction is worth £2m per annum to this organisation, then it is easy to see that this is a good investment.

Financial benefits are often called 'hard benefits', as opposed to non-financial or 'soft benefits'. Some benefits cannot be put into hard financial terms. It is still worth capturing them. You can argue the rights and wrongs for ever, but normally financial benefits tend to carry more weight in organisations' decision-making processes. However, there are many situations in which soft benefits will be the decisive information in approving a change initiative. This is often when the soft benefits are related to organisational strategy. So if your organisation's strategy is to increase the use of recycled materials, then irrespective of the financial case, there is a strong argument for any change initiative which will support this. It is therefore helpful to be aware of your organisation's strategy before clarifying all benefits.

Step 4.6 Build a business case

A plan shows what you want to do. To go from a plan to actively working on a change normally requires authorisation to spend the required money and use the necessary staff time. Most organisations require the development of a business case to gain this authorisation. The business case uses the information you have developed from planning, especially the understanding of costs and benefits.

A business case is a structured argument for an investment. Organisations use business cases to support decision making (and although it is titled a business case it is equally applicable to non-commercial organisations). A business case defines:

- Why you want to do something, which in this case is to achieve your change objective. Typically this is supported by some background information describing the rationale for the change.

- What will be required of your organisation to achieve this change. This can be primarily summarised by a high-level plan, the cost to perform the plan and list of resources needed.

- What the ongoing costs to the organisation will be once the change initiative is complete.

- The benefits you will gain by making this change, in both financial and non-financial terms.

- The alignment between this change initiative and your organisation's strategy.

- Any other information which is relevant or helpful to make a decision as to whether to invest in this change initiative or not.

Most organisations have formal business case processes and existing document templates which you can use. Normally there is a comparison between the costs and benefits in terms of a financial measure such as payback period or NPV (net present value).

Step 4.7 Gain approval to proceed

Gaining approval is normally about presenting your business case to the relevant level of senior management in your organisation. In the case of a change initiative there are three main audiences to seek approval from:

- *The change sponsor*: the change manager presents the initial business case and plan to the change sponsor.

- *The steering committee*: the change manager (with the change sponsor's support) presents the business case and plan to the steering committee.

- *Any general governance or authorisation levels*: the change sponsor presents (with the steering committee's support) to the appropriate decision-making group in the organisation. Most organisations have various defined authority levels for different levels of investment. So a very large investment may require main board approval, whilst a smaller investment will be approved by middle-level managers.

After discussing your plan and business case with each of these audiences you may be required to make amendments. Do not underestimate how long it can take to get approval for a major change initiative, and how much work it can be to revise the plan once you have had some feedback. It can take many months or even years(!) in some organisations for the largest of changes to be approved.

When you present a business case your first aim is to get approval for any investment. You should also try to get an explicit statement from the approvers of the priority of your initiative compared with others ongoing in the organisation. There is always more work around than people can complete, so it is helpful for your executives to state that your initiative has a high priority and people should give time to do the work required.

It is normally easier to gain approval for any investment if it is an already budgeted item. If it is not you will need to be willing to identify either what can be given up in a budget to cover the cost, or a really strong argument if you are looking for an increase in budget.

It is often helpful to consider the process of gaining approval for a change investment as a small project in its own right, especially if the resulting change is large or has a major impact. Before presenting a business case for any significant change it is worth warming up your audience in advance, so it roughly knows what you want to discuss with it and the size of the investment required. Surprising senior managers and executives with a request for major investment is a very good way to have your idea rejected!

Step 4.8 Implement quick wins

Once your change is approved you should start to implement any quick wins you have not yet started on. As soon as you have implemented them and start to see the benefits, make sure every relevant team and individual are aware of the benefits you have quickly achieved.

Quick wins will achieve little if they are not widely communicated. Communication is discussed more fully in step 8. Communicate loudly about your quick wins, but don't communicate about them for ever. Quick wins are refreshing and beneficial, but can also start to sound stale after a while.

Key tips

- The best plans are well thought through, but do not take for ever to create. This means you must balance your need for detail and accuracy with the length of time available for planning. Remember that the plan is meant to guide the change and enable you to manage it, not define every single activity that must be done on an hour-by-hour basis.

- Every plan must be specific to the project you are undertaking. By all means learn from old plans, but don't use them without adapting to the current situation.

- A plan is a statement of intentions, not an infallible prediction of what will happen. In all projects there has to be a willingness to adapt to reality, and, when appropriate, to change the plan.

- Look for and include quick wins in your plans. These speed delivery of benefits, and create a positive attitude to the change initiative.

- Don't forget to build any data collection activities into your plan.

- Be realistic in planning how long authorisations and approvals take in your organisation.

- Try to develop your business case in a format that your organisation is used to, and in the language of the organisation's strategy as this will ease gaining approval.

TO DO NOW

- Think about quick wins you can implement. Are there any obvious, simple improvements that can be made in the area of your change?

- If you do not know them, go and find your organisation's:

  - Financial approval levels and signoff authorities (who do you need to agree to your proposal before you can carry on?)

  - Business case templates and forms

  - Approval meeting schedule (if one exists).

- Clarify your organisation's strategy – is the change you are proposing aligned to this strategy or not? If not, does it really make sense to pursue it?

Step 5

Assess willingness and capability to change

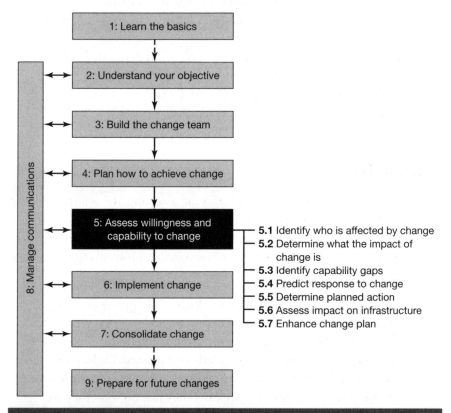

1: Learn the basics

2: Understand your objective

3: Build the change team

4: Plan how to achieve change

5: Assess willingness and capability to change

6: Implement change

7: Consolidate change

9: Prepare for future changes

8: Manage communications

5.1 Identify who is affected by change
5.2 Determine what the impact of change is
5.3 Identify capability gaps
5.4 Predict response to change
5.5 Determine planned action
5.6 Assess impact on infrastructure
5.7 Enhance change plan

THIS CHAPTER COVERS:

- An approach to assessing the capability to change, readiness for change, reactions to change, and planning the most appropriate resulting actions to ensure success.

THE CENTRAL POINT IS:

- Change does not occur in a vacuum, but must be designed to function with other components of your organisation. The people, processes, IT systems and infrastructure of your organisation must work with, or be capable of adapting to, the change proposed. Modify one component of your organisation, and every other component that interacts with the modified component needs to be reviewed to ensure it can still work in the same way. More than this, it is not just the capability to function with change that is important, but also the willingness of the people impacted to accept change. Change will always result in a reaction from people in the organisation. To optimise the outcome from a change situation you should determine who supports and who will resist the change, understand the underlying reasons why, and determine the most appropriate action to take in response to this reaction.

Setting the scene

To help to understand the criticality of assessing the willingness and capability to change, review the following four examples. Each shows a different aspect of reactions and results of change that has been ineffectively planned and managed, and has resulted in problems for the organisations involved:

1. A business wanted to increase its efficiency in processing orders. Many orders took a long time to process and were expensive to fulfil. Customers were waiting for extended periods to receive the products they wanted, and regularly complained. Orders were often cancelled. The sales force was highly critical of the order processing teams, often demanding, 'Why can't they just do what they are meant to do in the time required?' However, when the problem was analysed it was found that the root cause actually lay with the sales force. Sales personnel would fill in order forms quickly with a lot of missing or incorrect information, and would often put in special one-off changes in prices or product specifications to clinch a sale.

This left the order processing teams with a difficult and complex job. Lots of time was spent checking and correcting information, and many orders were effectively bespoke sales to a specific customer. Such bespoke products took a lot of time and expense to fulfil, and it was shown that product profitability was reduced by the lack of standardised products and by the number of orders cancelled. Previous efforts to get the sales force to improve the way it completed order forms and to limit the amount of product tailoring had floundered. The sales force was not really interested. Sales commission was related to sales made, and so when an order was raised the salesperson would get commission irrespective of the problems this caused elsewhere, and even irrespective if the order was ever completed. This was to be changed to a practice whereby a salesperson would only receive commission when the order was processed, and a log was kept of all rejected orders. Clear policy was defined describing how products and prices could be tailored and what could not be altered. Inconsistent orders would be rejected. Salespeople with a higher number of rejected orders would have their commission reduced. When the idea was proposed it was extremely unpopular with the sales teams, who said that they should focus on selling and not doing admin, adding, rather arrogantly, that they should not have to support incompetent clerical staff. The sales director's remuneration was linked to the total amount of sales commission paid and he also did not support the change. He fought aggressively against the change, telling the managing director that it would reduce revenues. With revenues at that time looking low anyway, the change was abandoned before it got started.

2. Two companies were merged to form a new, larger and potentially more successful business. The staff in the two companies had different contractual terms and conditions. The leadership team wanted to put everyone onto a common contract of work. The areas of contract that needed to be revised included the standard hours of work; the amount of holiday; health, travel and other benefits; sick policy; bonus levels; overtime and shift allowances; and various standard conditions of employment. The least contentious way to approach this would be to offer everyone a contract that took the best parts from the existing contracts, but when this was explored it was shown to be prohibitively expensive. The leadership team decided to

compromise: to be on average more generous than now (i.e. the total cost of employment for all staff would slightly increase), but some staff benefits would be reduced. The change was implemented, and the backlash from the staff was immediate. There was even a serious threat of strike action. The staff had been told that the merger was in everyone's interest, and yet many felt that the proposed changes to terms and conditions would be detrimental. They felt they had been lied to during the merger process. Calmly and rationally explaining the advantages of the change did not reduce the feelings of being cheated. To make things worse, and with unfortunate timing, the new bonus packages for the company's directors were announced at the same time. These were a significant increase on the bonus levels directors had previously received. Staff felt their benefits were declining while directors' were improving. The change was pushed through and strikes were avoided. But for many months afterwards there was a significant level of bad feeling, sickness rates were considerably higher, and staff turnover increased substantially.

3. A telecommunications business wanted to replace its customer care and billing system with a new computer system that would enable it to provide much better customer support, and have the capability to respond more rapidly to other changes in future, such as launching new products. Customer care and billing systems lie at the heart of the operations of any telecoms company. These are highly complex systems that are difficult to get perfectly right, but in this case the technical development was done exceptionally well. A full analysis of requirements was done beforehand and the software was tailored precisely to the business's specific needs. The new computer system was fully tested and seemed to be implemented successfully with very few faults. It was only in the following weeks after implementation that many problems arose. A few people in one of the operational departments, whose work was affected by the new system, did not seem to know that a new system was being implemented. Some staff in call centres knew of the change, but did not understand how it would affect them. They tried to work in the same way they had before. This was no longer possible, and they could not complete their normal tasks easily. Others, in the finance department, had not been trained fully to use the system. Overall, although the new computer system worked well, the lack of

understanding and preparedness for it caused a major disruption to the business which took months to recover from.

4. A business, with a large field force of engineers who installed and fixed equipment in consumers' homes, decided it was time to buy new vans for its staff. The engineers were based in a series of depots across the country which they would go to every day and stock up their vans. The existing vans were reaching the end of their lives, and additionally were becoming too small for the range of equipment the engineers increasingly had to carry. A new van was selected and over the coming months the old fleet was replaced. The new van was wider and longer, and critically higher than existing vans – the larger volume gave plenty of room to carry the full range of stock the engineers required, and even left some space for growth. The new vans were a success, until the time to replace the vans for the engineers based in West London. About 10% of these engineers had a home base in the West London area, but no one had considered the unique features of the garage facilities in that location. Due to the high cost of property, garage space was limited and of restricted height. The new vans would not easily fit into these garages, and, because of the height restriction, could not be backed up close to the warehouse doors. The result was that engineers had to carry stock for their vans from the warehouse to a car park about 50 metres away. This was a slight health and safety risk, and it also added significantly to the time the engineers had to spend loading and unloading every morning. Eventually, and at some cost, the new vans were abandoned in the West London area and a different, lower van was chosen for just that area.

Each of these examples shows different consequences of changes which have been ineffectively planned for and managed, and have resulted in problems for the organisations involved.

The first two show the human response to change. In the first example the sales force pushes back and stops a change. The change is in the best interests of the organisation, but it is not to the personal advantage of sales staff. Sales are normally a powerful part of any commercial organisation. Where changes are disadvantageous to any powerful group you have to expect at least a negative response, and possibly active attempts to stop the change. There are several strategies to overcome such a response.

You can try to educate the teams about the wider benefit to the organisation as a whole. Showing sales staff how the costs of the business are reduced when the complexity of products is decreased will convince some of them to support the change. Also, you could try to find ways to align the interests of the negative group with the change. In this case the sales force could be educated to see that if orders were correctly done, and so could be processed quickly, customers would be happier and it would be easier to win repeat sales. Critically, you have to find other powerful supporters of the change to help you push it through. When the sales director tells the MD that this is a bad change, you need someone of at least the same seniority to convince the MD why the change is a good thing.

The second example is slightly different as the response to the change comes after the change has been made and not before. Real care is needed when making changes which affect large numbers of staff. The risk of a negative response is not just to the success of the change you are making, but also to the operations of your organisation. If people really did go on strike then any savings made by reducing staff benefits might soon look small compared with the losses from not being able to operate at all. Costs from increases in sickness levels or higher rates of staff turnover tend to be less obvious than those from a strike, and it is almost impossible to understand fully the cost of a reduction in motivation. But be in no doubt: such factors have a significant and lasting cost. In this example, better communication and expectation setting could probably have solved the problem. Most people are reasonable, and will accept a reasonable argument. Showing that you cannot simply increase everyone's benefits to a level you could not afford, listening to staff suggestions about what parts to increase and what benefits they would accept a reduction in, explaining that on average staff are actually better off, would all have helped to reduce the problem. Additionally, during the merger the communications made to staff could have been tailored so they did not feel later that they were lied to. Finally, the timing of the announcement on director's bonuses was insensitive and bound to cause comparisons. It should have been delayed.

The third scenario is quite different. This example is not about people's response, but about organisational readiness for and capability to make a change. Organisations are not built up from a set of discrete components that work independently, but are complex systems of interdependency.

Change one component and this will impact on others. In this example, a lot of effort was put into making the best possible IT system for customer care and billing. That is good, but it is simply not enough. Everyone whose work touches or is touched by the customer care and billing system should have been identified, had the changes explained, and in many cases should have had proper training on how it differed from previous IT systems. As it was, the staff did not have the capability, knowledge or processes to operate effectively with the new IT system. New processes should have been designed to work with this system. Inadequate organisational readiness for change, especially change associated with new computer systems or launching new products, is often a cause of major operational problems.

The final example is yet another aspect of change management, and this is about the technical integration of changes into the existing infrastructure of an organisation. This is related to organisational readiness, but instead of asking *who* needs to work in a different way following a change, it asks *what* is affected by a change. In the example, a vehicle has to be able to fit within the height of a warehouse. The impact of change upon the infrastructure of an organisation often strays into specialised, technical subjects, such as systems integration, which are beyond the scope of this book. However, the basic principles are touched upon, and in many cases thinking through these principles will avoid potential problems. A very common area in which an organisation's infrastructure must be adapted is that of IT systems. If an IT system is changed any other computer system it interfaces with may have to be adapted. But buildings, machinery or any other part of your infrastructure may also be affected by a change.

Introduction to assessing willingness and capability to change

Project management methodologies and general management tend to focus on task completion and achieving a result at a point in time. What differentiates change management is the strong focus on ensuring that the changes work on an ongoing basis in the real world and are accepted by the people who have to live with the changes. Change managers should be less focused on the end point of their current change project than on how the organisation will work after the change has been made.

To understand how an organisation will work once a change initiative is finished, change managers must assess and plan action from three perspectives:

- *Human response to change*: every change will create a response from the people it affects. Sometimes this response is positive and supports the change; sometimes it is negative and will push against the change. This response will come into effect not only when a change is implemented, but can start as soon as a change is even considered. Change management has to plan for and deal with this response, which can not only disrupt work on the change initiative, but also in more severe cases disrupt the whole operation of your organisation. Business history is full of many cases of staff deliberately vandalising key equipment and computers as a response to change that was detrimental to them.

- *Organisational readiness for change*: if a change is to be successfully implemented the appropriate people in the organisation must be capable of working in the changed way. They must be aware of the change, understand it, and where necessary be trained to work and behave in a different manner.

- *Integration of change into existing infrastructure*: if you want to change any component of your organisation, you have to consider how this component interacts and works with other components of your organisation. It is like replacing a cog in a watch. If a cog wears out a new cog can be put in, but only if it fits with all the others – or if the others are also changed to fit with it.

By looking from each of these three angles you will take the broader set of implications from change into account, and reduce the risk associated with change. Let's consider each of these in more detail.

Human response to change

If organisations did not employ anyone, and simply consisted of machines and computer systems, change would be much simpler and easier. There are a series of technical difficulties with adapting machines and computer systems, but no machine is going to feel hurt if you decide to change what you use it for, or go on strike if you decide to remove it altogether from your organisation. Machines do not have emotions and do not try to interpret what is happening around them. They do not respond in a negative or positive way when you make modifications. You can do what you like with them!

There are many practical, ethical, personal, legal and regulatory reasons for not treating people in the same way as machines. From a practical perspective, you want to motivate staff to feel positive, and to avoid aggravating them. Motivated staff are more creative, productive and reliable; aggravated staff tend not to be. At the extreme, unhappy staff can strike, but more often dissatisfaction results in other, more subtle losses in productivity. Morally and ethically, we each have some core beliefs and values about how we want to be treated and how we feel we should treat others. These beliefs and values are meaningless if you do not apply them at work. Organisations often have implicit and explicit values as well. Organisational values, such as a commitment to treat staff with respect, are worthless if these are not reflected in the way change is managed. There are many pieces of law which relate to the way people have to be treated, and regulations which control factors such as how and when staff must be informed of certain changes. The implications of ignoring such laws and regulations can be serious.

The world of management literature is full of many case studies of benign change being so badly managed that it has resulted in major difficulties within organisations and permanently damaged relationships between organisational leaders and staff. In contrast, there are plenty of examples of difficult and unpopular change being managed so well that if people are not exactly cheering when it occurs, they accept it without any disruption to the organisation. This is achieved by preparing for and dealing with people's response to change.

Change will only happen if the pressure for change is greater than the resistance to it. By working to understand the resistance and taking action to minimise it, the likelihood of successful change is increased significantly.

Reactions to change can be infinitely varied, but can be summarised as three main types of reaction. They may be more or less positive about a change, which will typically make the process of implementation easier. They may be more or less negative, which will typically make the process of implementation harder. More subtly they may be neutral to change.

Sometimes the biggest problem in a change situation is a lack of reaction. If people are completely passive it can be difficult to implement some types of change, as some change requires the active involvement of staff to be successful.

A simple model of change shows that you should leverage positive responses to change, and either convince those with negative responses that they are wrong, or somehow neutralise any action they take as a result of negative feelings. The reality is often more complex than this, as resistance to change can sometimes be perfectly valid. It may not be the response that is a problem, but the change itself. Even very experienced managers are capable of identifying and pursuing bad changes, and it is right that staff resist the change. One valid outcome from resistance is therefore to modify change proposals. On the other hand, even if the change is the right thing to do, it will create a negative response from individuals for whom it is detrimental. The way the change is announced and explained, and the way the organisation supports and incentivises staff suffering from detrimental change, have a significant impact on their responses, and can change confrontational situations into a constructive interaction in which even staff losing their roles will work hard until they leave the organisation.

When thinking about reactions to change it is important to avoid simplistic thinking. Often arguments about change are seen as issues between management and workers. Although choosing a path for change is often a leadership and management decision, and some response will come from the staff at lower levels in a hierarchy, people at all levels in an organisation may perceive themselves as winners or losers from change. Some of the most helpful people in change situations are motivated and excited junior staff. In contrast, some of the most difficult problems arise when very senior managers or executives oppose a change. I have seen no evidence, nor do I believe, that senior-level staff are any more rational, consistent or generally helpful in assessing change and in their response towards it.

Another type of simplistic thinking to avoid is seeing the management of people's reactions as an issue to be resolved purely by rational argument. Being logically and rationally right is not always enough to convince people of the benefits of change. We are not purely rational animals who make decisions and respond based on a logical assessment of a situation. We respond according to perceptions and emotions. Change managers have to be able to deal with non-rational arguments and often successful change happens because arguments are made at an emotional level. Think of your own experience: do you respond more positively to the dry, logical presentation of the finance director explaining great financial results, or to professional communication events with an upbeat atmosphere, supported with optimistic music, lights and positive images, when you get a sense of excitement from working in your organisation?

A common trap to avoid is creating resistance to change by presenting the change, either deliberately or accidentally, as a criticism of past ways of working. Change brings in new ways of working, but it also means stopping some existing ways of working. Often people resist change because they have pride in their work, and being asked to do something different is perceived as a criticism. This can be avoided by respecting people's need to feel valued, and ensuring that it is clear that the change is not a criticism of past work. The past ways of working were appropriate for yesterday, but are no longer appropriate for the requirements of today. Individuals' skills and efforts are still wanted, just in a different way.

Finally, resistance often comes about through a lack of involvement in change. People are much more likely to accept change when they have a sense of ownership for the change, which is developed through involvement in the design and implementation of change. This is a good reason to have as broad a change team as possible. Where change is designed separately from the staff working in current ways, the staff are much more likely to reject the change, even if it is fundamentally good. In contrast, even the most difficult to accept change will be accepted with sufficient staff involvement.

The process of determining how people may react to change and taking appropriate action is one of the key aspects of change management. Change management uses the positive reactions to help implementation, and takes action to counter negative reactions to avoid barriers to implementation. This makes change management a powerful methodology for altering the way people work and interact, and not just another project management approach.

The starting point for dealing with people's response to change is to try to predict it. Of course you cannot literally analyse change from the viewpoint of every individual in the company (although you can train your managers to do this across your organisation), but you have to look at key groups and the powerful individuals whose response you have to predict, manage and influence. Understanding people's reaction to change requires a real ability to listen. Great change managers are constantly alert, and deliberately seek opportunities to understand people's feelings about change.

Organisational readiness for change

Preparation of all the people in your organisation who will be affected by change is key to success. How much people need to be prepared depends on the specific change. It can vary from a need for general awareness that something is happening, to a requirement for significant training. The underlying principle is that for change to work, the organisation must be ready and capable of changing.

In order for people to be fully prepared for a new change there are many activities that have to be done. In summary, the main tasks to undertake are to:

- Communicate regularly to ensure staff are aware of the change. Unexpected change, even if it is completely benign, will result in unnecessary resistance.

- Explain the change to ensure staff fully understand the change. It is one thing to know about a change, it is quite another to really understand it. As a simple example, I know an automatic car is different from a manual one, but until I have been in one and driven it I will not really understand the difference.

- Analyse and assess the impact of the change upon staff. By this I mean having a real understanding of how the change will affect the working life of every member of staff. Following the change, will they have to work differently? Will they have to have new knowledge? Will they need different IT systems and tools? Will they have to behave differently or interact with customers in a different way?

- Adapt any working practices, processes or policies to be consistent with the change. The change may be about new processes, but even if it is not it will often result in a need to change processes or procedures. For example, a change introducing a new IT system, or launching a new product in a business, will require new processes for people who have to work with the IT system or support the new product.

- Make sure that everyone can work to the new practices, processes or policies and whatever else is changed. This is normally about education and training, but it may also be about replacing staff if the skills required to perform a role change significantly.

Integration of change into existing infrastructure

Your organisation is not built only from the people it employs. It is made up of a range of infrastructure components. In this context I use the word 'infrastructure' to mean all components of your organisation except for the staff. I include IT systems, buildings, machinery, vehicles – the list is virtually endless depending on the specific nature of your organisation. Your infrastructure is essential to the successful operation of your organisation, and has to be able to continue to support your organisation following a change.

In reality, in most change situations, many components of your infrastructure will not be affected. However, if it is not considered your infrastructure is often the area that can throw up unpleasant surprises. Decisions over very mundane-sounding topics like power supplies and sufficient floor space in offices are normally peripheral to change initiatives – but find out unexpectedly that you need extra power or greater floor space and you may find your change project delayed by months and even years as the need is fulfilled.

Making sure your infrastructure is ready for change can be complex. An organisation is not made of discrete, independent components, but an infrastructure that is built up over time and operates as one working system. It may not be a seamless system, or even the most efficient or effective system, but any change risks disrupting the system and making things worse unless it is fully thought through. Most infrastructures have not been developed to a single plan, and are not like a series of Lego

STEP 5: ASSESS WILLINGNESS AND CAPABILITY TO CHANGE

blocks where you can simply pull out a red block and replace it with a blue one; the boundaries are not so clear cut. Most infrastructures can be disrupted in unexpected places with poorly executed change. Understanding the impact of change on your infrastructure is easiest when you involve people who really understand your specific environment and how component A links to or is dependent on component B, and therefore can identify that if component A is adapted what also must be modified in component B.

For IT systems (and some other engineered components of some organisations' infrastructures), there is a special discipline called *systems integration* which is used to ensure that different components of a system can work together. Systems integration relies on having an understanding of your systems architecture. A 'systems architecture' is a representation of how the components of your IT systems all fit together. Systems integration is a specialised discipline, but the basic principle – that the components of a system cannot be built in isolation, but have to be designed, developed, tested and implemented to work together as a working system – is not difficult to understand.

The step-by-step guide
STEP 5 – Assess willingness and capability to change

Step 5.1 Identify who is affected by change

Here step 5 starts by checking whether your organisation is both capable and willing to change by identifying two groups of people: those *who will be affected by the change* and those *who might have an impact on the change*.

In using the phrase '*who will be affected by the change*', I mean the people who, as a result of the change, will have to work or behave differently, or simply need to know about the change to continue to perform their role. In using the phrase '*who might have an impact on the change*', I mean the people who, whether or not they are directly impacted by the change, have either the power or influence to affect your ability to implement the change, and have the inclination to use this power or influence. In other words, these are the people who might support or oppose the change.

For a significant change these definitions can include practically anyone in your organisation. If you are a large organisation this could be thousands of people, and you cannot possibly analyse centrally the needs, motives and intentions of so many. Therefore you have to be pragmatic and seek to identify all the main groups of staff affected by the change. Additionally, you should try to identify key individuals in positions of power and influence who may have an impact on the change. This is most usually senior managers and executives, but can include other influential people such as union representatives.

A good way to do this is to put together a small group of key individuals to review the change. To carry out this review ideally requires a selection of people who understand the way the organisation works, and who know who its key people are. Depending on the nature of your change and the people involved, this may be an open session, or may have to be treated with great sensitivity. By asking the questions below, you will start to develop a good understanding of who is affected by a change:

- *Key processes*: which processes or procedures are altered by the change, and which groups interact with these processes and procedures?
- *Organisation chart*: which teams or departments will be altered by the change, by having to work differently or having their roles and responsibilities modified?
- *IT systems*: which IT systems will be altered by the change, and who uses them?
- *Infrastructure*: what parts of your infrastructure will be altered by the change and who does this affect?
- *Who can have an impact on change*: are there any individuals or groups who are likely to have any negative or positive influence on the change?
- *Who else might be concerned about the change:* is there any group that is not affected, but might assume it is? (For example, because the group performs a role very similar to another team which is affected.)

Such a review will tend to focus on the staff in your organisation. Before you finish the review it is worth asking yourself if there are people external to your organisation whom you must also consider. Most changes are only relevant to the staff of the organisation, but some changes have wider implications. A change in a university is relevant to the students as well as to direct employees. A change which radically changes a business's profitability or costs is relevant to shareholders as well as managers. A change to the services of a charity is relevant to the donors and recipients of charitable services as well as the charity's staff. In each case simply thinking about the staff of the organisation is not enough really to understand the impact of the change.

The output from this step should be a list of departments and individuals, and perhaps some external groups. There is a balance to find in terms of the level of detail to minimise complexity and workload, whilst covering all aspects of the change. One way to look at this is by considering what the impact is. If there are different parts of the group for whom the impact is different then you have to break the group into its constituent parts. Where the impact on the group is the same for all members of the group, leave it as one group.

Let's now work up to the first example from the start of this chapter. In this example a company wanted to improve efficiency in processing orders, having found that the root cause of current problems lies with the sales force in filling in order forms with insufficient care and quality, and also offering too many variations in products to customers. You will recall that the proposed change sought to change the behaviour of sales by modifying the way commissions were paid and the rules for accepting or rejecting orders. The teams and individuals most affected by this change are shown in Table 5.1.

The approach shown in this book describes change being driven by an individual change manager supported by a change team. The change manager and the change team come together temporarily for the life of the change initiative, like any other project team. This is a great way to manage most changes. However, for the largest of business transformations a central change team alone will not be able to assess and manage the impact across all the staff in the organisation. The change team therefore has to rely on every line manager to do part of the role of

	Teams affected by change
1	Sales account managers
2	Sales management (i.e. the managers of the sales account managers)
3	Sales director
4	Order processing
5	Operations director (in whose domain order processing lies)
6	Product management
7	Customer service
8	Customers
9	Finance
10	Other members of the leadership team (excluding the sales and operations directors)

Table 5.1   **Sample list of teams affected by change**

the change team, especially those tasks associated with assessing the impact on individuals and teams across the organisation, determining the necessary response and actions required to manage this impact, implementing the identified actions, and supporting the individuals in their team through the change.

For these largest and most complex transformation projects the whole management team effectively becomes part of the supporting change team, or put another way, implementing the change becomes a part of the day-to-day work of all managers. This is one step on the way to moving between treating change as a transactional activity that occurs from time to time, and regarding change as a continuous part of the organisation's work. This is put in context in the Appendix.

Where change is regarded as a continuous and ongoing part of every manager's role there is still a place for a change manager and change team to co-ordinate complex changes, but every line manager has a role in supporting every change and every manager needs change management awareness and training.

Step 5.2 Determine what the impact of change is

Now you have the list of affected teams and individuals, you next need to expand the information by documenting the nature of the impact. Table 5.2 expands on Table 5.1 by answering the question 'What precisely will be different for the individual or teams you have identified following the implementation of the change?' Whilst the information at this stage does not need to be very detailed, you must try to be as specific as possible. This is best shown through an example.

	Affected teams	Nature of impact
1	Sales account manager	Must complete order forms with greater accuracy Can promise faster orders and fewer rejects Restricted range of tailoring of prices or products Commission directly affected by quality of work as well as volume of sales as measured by order reject percentage Commissioned on order completion, not order entry (May create initial delay in paying commission on changeover)
2	Sales management	Need to change approach to managing and coaching staff to focus on sales quality as well as sales volumes Potentially have to deal with disgruntled sales staff and support change that they personally do not like Reduced bonus if sales decline/but should also be an opportunity for increased bonus
3	Sales director	Will be assessed against order reject levels and customer cancellation levels as well as total sales value Potentially has to deal with disgruntled sales management and supporting change that they personally do not like Reduced bonus if sales decline/but should also be an opportunity for increased bonus if sales increase
4	Order processing	Tighter working rules Greater power to reject orders which do not conform to rules Less time spent resolving unusual or problematical orders

	Affected teams	Nature of impact
5	Operations director	Faster order throughput, fewer escalated issues to resolve Fewer complaints about order processing team Generally better staff satisfaction in order processing team
6	Product management	Products sold aligned to product definitions Increased product profitability makes it easier to hit own performance targets Less time spent analysing and fulfilling once-off customer orders
7	Customer service	Customer queries on status of orders reduced as orders will be fulfilled more quickly and hence fewer customers will ring in Customer queries about product range and options initially may increase
8	Customers	Faster order processing Fewer rejected orders Reduced level of product tailoring possible
9	Finance	Will be asked to change commission structure to pay on order completion, not order entry, and to reflect reject levels Need to track order reject levels by salesperson and overall customer order cancellation rate Claw-back on commission needs to be implemented
10	Other members of the leadership team (excluding the sales and operations director)	No significant impact, but may have to be able to describe change and rationale for change to staff and customers Need to provide resources to work on change initiative

Table 5.2 **Sample list of teams affected by change**

Step 5.3 Identify capability gaps

The information collected in step 5.2 should be extended by adding the capability gaps of the groups identified (Table 5.3). A capability gap is where the change requires staff to work in a way which they do not currently have the capability to do.

	Affected teams	Nature of impact	Capability gaps	Other ongoing changes
1	Sales account managers	Must complete order forms with greater accuracy Can promise faster orders and fewer rejects Restricted range of tailoring of prices or products Commission directly affected by quality of work as well as volume of sales as measured by order reject percentage Commission on order completion, not order entry. (May create initial delay in paying commission on changeover)	Do not have full understanding of how to complete order forms correctly Do not know new product and pricing policy Need way to convince customers to buy product when there are reduced options to tailor product	Major sale push being lined up with advertising campaign in April/May
2	Sales management	Need to change approach to managing and coaching staff to focus on sales quality as well as sales volumes Potentially have to deal with disgruntled sales staff and support change that they personally do not like Reduced bonus if sales decline/but should also be an opportunity for increased bonus	Need ability to support and explain new policy, why it is being done and benefits for account managers Need ability to support and manage account managers to work to new policy	Major sales push being lined up with advertising campaign in April/May

▶

123

	Impacted teams	Nature of impact	Capability gaps	Other changes ongoing
3	Sales director	Will be assessed against order reject levels and customer cancellation levels as well as total sales value Potentially has to deal with disgruntled sales management and supporting change that they personally do not like Reduced bonus if sales decline/ but should also be an opportunity for increased bonus if sales increase	Needs revised performance metrics to manage department	
4	Order processing	Tighter working rules Greater power to reject orders which do not conform to rules Less time spent resolving unusual or problematical orders	Understanding of revised rejection rules and what to do if an order does not conform Ability to reject and log rejection of unsuitable orders	
5	Operations director	Faster order throughput, fewer escalated issues to resolve Fewer complaints about order processing team Generally better staff satisfaction in order processing team	Needs new performance metrics to manage department Speed to deliver orders and customer cancellation rates	
6	Product management	Products sold aligned to product definitions Increased product profitability makes it easier to hit own performance targets	(None identified)	New range of products being launched at same time, so product teams very busy Support for advertising push in April/May

7	Customer service	Less time spent analysing and fulfilling once-off customer orders Customer queries on status of orders reduced as orders will be fulfilled more quickly and hence fewer customers will ring in Customer queries about product range and options initially may increase	Understanding of product and pricing policy	It's proposed to move the customer service department to a new building some time in Q3. While this is happening it will not be able to work on any other changes
8	Customers	Faster order processing Fewer rejected orders Reduced level of product tailoring possible	Understanding of product and pricing policy	
9	Finance	Will be asked to change commission structure to pay on order completion, not order entry, and to reflect reject levels Need to track order reject levels by salesperson and overall customer order cancellation rate Claw-back on commission needs to be implemented	Understanding of order rejection policy Understanding of new commission basis Ability to claw back commission	Finance systems upgrades being implemented in June, during which time it will not be possible to make changes to commission structures
10	Other members of the leadership team (excluding the sales and operations director)	No significant impact, but may have to be able to describe change and rationale for change to staff and customers Need to provide resources to work on change initiative	Full understanding of the change, its implications and the underlying rationale	Significant other change work being driven by new corporate strategy following board review

Table 5.3 **Sample list of teams affected by change**

To complete this information, ask: to work or behave in the way proposed, what do staff need that they do not already have? This may be as simple as an awareness of some activity, but it could be specific knowledge and understanding or new skills. It can also include the need for new tools, often including new IT systems.

Additionally, at this stage you should start to gain an understanding of what other changes the groups identified are being subjected to at present. If people are working on many other changes in parallel they may not have the time to work on yours. Also, people have a limited ability to absorb change at any one time. Trying to implement too much change in parallel tends to result in less successful change.

Step 5.4 Predict response to change

Now that you have an understanding of how change is likely to affect different groups and individuals in your organisation it is time to predict what sort of response they will have to the proposed change.

This is not about trying to guess the reaction of every individual in your organisation, but trying to forecast how the main groups and key individuals will respond. The way to approach this is to ask two related, but subtly different, questions:

● Who are the winners and losers from the change – and how are they most likely to respond?
● Who might interpret themselves to be winners and losers from the change?

Table 5.4 continues the example.

	Affected teams	Nature of impact	Capability gaps	Other ongoing changes	Expected response
1	Sales account managers	Must complete order forms with greater accuracy Can promise faster orders and fewer rejects Restricted range of tailoring of prices or products Commission directly affected by quality of work as well as volume of sales as measured by order reject percentage Commission on order completion, not order entry. (May create initial delay in paying commission on changeover)	Do not have full understanding of how to complete order forms correctly Do not know new product and pricing policy Need way to convince customers to buy product when there are reduced options to tailor product	Major sale push being lined up with advertising campaign in April/May	*Negative:* will see this as a threat and likely to reduce their sales commission in short run. We may see increase in staff turnover from those who do not like new rules
2	Sales management	Need to change approach to managing and coaching staff to focus on sales quality as well as sales volumes Potentially have to deal with disgruntled sales staff and support change that they personally do not like Reduced bonus if sales decline/but should also be an opportunity for increased bonus	Need ability to support and explain new policy, why it is being done and benefits for account managers Need ability to support and manage account managers to work to new policy	Major sales push being lined up with advertising campaign in April/May	*Negative:* will see this as a threat to current commission levels, and also make job harder by annoying sales force

▶

Affected teams	Nature of impact	Capability gaps	Other ongoing changes	Expected response
3 Sales director	Will be assessed against order reject levels and customer cancellation levels as well as total sales value Potentially has to deal with disgruntled sales management and supporting change that they personally do not like Reduced bonus if sales decline/but should also be an opportunity for increased bonus if sales increase	Needs revised performance metrics to manage department		*Negative/neutral:* although the sales director knows this is the right thing to do he or she may see it as negative as in the short run it may reduce his or her personal bonus levels
4 Order processing	Tighter working rules Greater power to reject orders which do not conform to rules Less time spent resolving unusual or problematical orders	Understanding of revised rejection rules and what to do if an order does not conform Ability to reject and log rejection of unsuitable orders		*Generally positive:* mainly will see change as positive as will ease work significantly May be partly negative as could interpret becoming more clerical and less creative/decision making. Also may see reduction in work as a threat to jobs
5 Operations director	Faster order throughput, fewer escalated issues to resolve Fewer complaints about order processing team Generally better staff satisfaction in order processing team	Needs new performance metrics to manage department. Speed to deliver orders and customer cancellation rates		*Positive:* removes root cause of a major problem and he or she can now focus on managing department better

6	Product management	Products sold aligned to product definitions. Increased product profitability makes it easier to hit own performance targets. Less time spent analysing and fulfilling once-off customer orders	[None identified]	New range of products being launched at same time, so product teams very busy. Support for advertising push in April/May	*Positive*: increases product profitability and reduces work spent delivering once-off products to customers
7	Customer service	Customer queries on status of orders reduced as orders will be fulfilled more quickly and hence fewer customers will ring in. Customer queries about product range and options initially may increase	Understanding of product and pricing policy	It's proposed to move the customer service department to a new building some time in Q3. While this is happening it will not be able to work on any other changes	*Neutral*: will probably prefer new basis as customer queries will be simpler to handle. May see reduced customer queries as a threat to some jobs
8	Customers	Faster order processing. Fewer rejected orders. Reduced level of product tailoring possible	Understanding of product and pricing policy		*Mixed*: many customers will like improved order processing times, but those who expect significant tailoring of products may be disappointed with new policy to limit tailoring

Affected teams	Nature of impact	Capability gaps	Other ongoing changes	Expected response
9 Finance	Will be asked to change commission structure to pay on order completion, not order entry, and to reflect reject levels Need to track order reject levels by salesperson and overall customer order cancellation rate Claw-back on commission needs to be implemented	Understanding of order rejection policy Understanding of new commission basis Ability to claw back commission	Finance systems upgrades being implemented in June, during which time it will not be possible to make changes to commission structures	*Positive*: the change will increase product profitability, and finance will generally perceive this as the right thing to do
10 Other members of the leadership team (excluding the sales and operations directors)	No significant impact, but may have to be able to describe change and rationale for change to staff and customers Need to provide resources to work on change initiative	Full understanding of the change, its implications and the underlying rationale	Significant other change work being driven by new corporate strategy following board review	*Positive/neutral*: the change will increase overall profitability, but this effect may be hidden amongst the effect of all the other ongoing projects across business

Table 5.4 **Sample list of teams affected by change**

Step 5.5 Determine planned action

Now you have a good piece of analysis telling you how people will be affected by a change, and how they may respond to the change. Change management is not simply about collecting information so you have an understanding of your environment – it is about taking action to ensure the change is a success. Therefore you have to decide what actions you are going to take as a result of the information you have gathered (Table 5.5).

The information in Table 5.5 shows a much better understanding of the change and the necessary actions. It is worth reviewing all the information, and seeing if it alters your attitude to the change. In step 4 (plan how to achieve change), you built a business case for your change, and gained approval to undertake it. This business case was built mainly as a comparison of costs and benefits. Now you have a much better understanding of your organisation's capability and willingness to change. If you review this information you will start to understand the risk associated with your change. If your assessment shows that work needs to be done, but essentially the organisation is capable and willing to make the change, then the risk is low. On the other hand, if your organisation is neither capable nor willing to make a change, the risk of failure is higher.

Discuss your assessment with the change sponsor. Is he or she willing to bear this risk? Does the sponsor think you need to get wider approval and revisit the business case now that you understand the risk better? Is the change going to have such a big impact that you need approval beyond those who originally approved the business case?

	Affected teams	Nature of impact	Capability gaps	Other ongoing changes	Expected response	Proposed actions
1	Sales account managers	Must complete order forms with greater accuracy	Do not have full understanding of how to complete order forms correctly	Major sales push being lined up with advertising campaign in April/May	*Negative:* Will see this as a threat and likely to reduce their sales commission in short run. We may see increase in staff turnover from those who do not like new rules	Develop communications material explaining benefits of change
		Can promise faster orders and fewer rejects	Do not know new product and pricing policy			Communicate to sales, and run listening sessions to gather comments, concerns and suggestions
		Restricted range of tailoring of prices or products	Need way to convince customers to buy product when there are reduced options to tailor product			Respond to comments, concerns and suggestions
		Commission directly impacted by quality of work as well as volume of sales as measured by order reject percentage				Modify sales collateral and key sales messages to support new approach
		Commission on order completion, not order entry (May create initial delay in paying commission on changeover)				Develop training sessions for new policy and sales messages
						Plan and roll out training
						Prepare HR for recruitment as a result of increased turnover
						Plan staggered rollout of commission so sales are not initially out of pocket

2	Sales management	Need to change approach to managing and coaching staff to focus on sales quality as well as sales volumes Potentially have to deal with disgruntled sales staff and support change that they personally do not like Reduced bonus if sales decline/but should also be an opportunity for increased bonus	Need ability to support and explain new policy, why it is being done and benefits for account managers Need ability to support and manage account managers to work to new policy	Major sales push being lined up with advertising campaign in April/May	*Negative:* Will see this as a threat to current commission levels, and also make job harder by annoying sales force	Develop communications material explaining benefits of change Provide support for education of sales Closely monitor to ensure sales management are enforcing and encouraging adherence by the sales account managers to the new policy
3	Sales director	Will be assessed against order reject levels and customer cancellation levels as well as total sales value Potentially has to deal with disgruntled sales management and supporting change that they personally do not like	Needs revised performance metrics to manage department		*Negative/neutral:* Although the sales director knows this is the right thing to do he or she may see it as negative as in the short run it may reduce his or her personal bonus levels	Develop communications material explaining benefits of change Provide support for education of sales and sales management Develop new management information to provide new performance data on an ongoing basis

►

Affected teams	Nature of impact	Capability gaps	Other ongoing changes	Expected response	Proposed actions
3 Sales director *continued*	Reduced bonus if sales decline/but should also be an opportunity for increased bonus if sales increase				
4 Order processing	Tighter working rules Greater power to reject orders which do not conform to rules Less time spent resolving unusual or problematical orders	Understanding of revised rejection rules and what to do if an order does not conform Ability to reject and log rejection of unsuitable orders		*Generally positive:* mainly will see change as positive as will ease work significantly May be partly negative as could interpret becoming more clerical and less creative/decision making. Also may see reduction in work as a threat to jobs.	Develop communications material explaining benefits of change Communicate to order processing, and run listening sessions to gather comments, concerns and suggestions Respond to comments, concerns and suggestions New order policy guidelines Review existing processes and amend to fit with new policy Develop training material to ensure order teams understand and are capable of implementing policy Roll out training

#	Stakeholder	Benefits	Needs	Considerations	Assessment	Actions
5	Operations director	Faster order throughput, fewer escalated issues to resolve. Fewer complaints about order processing team. Generally better staff satisfaction in order processing team	Needs new performance metrics to manage department. Speed to deliver orders and customer cancellation rates		*Positive*: Removes root cause of a major problem to rightful home and can now focus on managing department better	Ensure actively supports and sponsors change and is countering any negative communication from sales area. Implement regular update session on project progress. Develop new management information to provide new performance data on an ongoing basis
6	Product management	Products sold aligned to product definitions. Increased product profitability makes it easier to hit own performance targets. Less time spent analysing and fulfilling once-off customer orders	[None identified]	New range of products being launched at same time, so product teams very busy. Support for advertising push in April/May	*Positive*: Increases product profitability and reduces work spent delivering once-off products to customers	Develop product/price policy and product/price tailoring rules. The advertising push in April/May must not be adversely affected by these changes, so they should be fully implemented by then
7	Customer service	Customer queries on status of orders reduced as orders will be fulfilled more quickly and hence fewer customers will ring in	Understanding of product and pricing policy	It's proposed to move the customer service department to a new building some time in Q3. While this is happening it will not be able to work on any other changes	*Neutral*: Will probably prefer new basis as customer queries will be simpler to handle. May see reduced customer queries as a threat to some jobs	General communication on proposed changes to customer services. Review customer handling scripts and procedures, and ensure they are compliant with new product policy

▶

	Affected teams	Nature of impact	Capability gaps	Other ongoing changes	Expected response	Proposed actions
7	Customer service *continued*	Customer queries about product range and options initially may increase				Develop training material to ensure order teams understand and are capable of implementing policy Roll out training
8	Customers	Faster order processing Fewer rejected orders Reduced level of product tailoring possible	Understanding of product and pricing policy		*Mixed:* Many customers will like improved order processing times, but those who expect significant tailoring of products may be disappointed with new policy to limit tailoring	Marketing communication explaining product changes and benefits to customers Review pricing – potentially reduce to reflect the now standardised product set Run some focus groups to capture customer responses and amend product tailoring rules accordingly
9	Finance	Will be asked to change commission structure to pay on order completion, not order entry, and to reflect reject levels	Understanding of order rejection policy Understanding of new commission basis Ability to claw back commission	Finance systems upgrades being implemented in June, during which time it will not be possible to make changes to commission structures	*Positive:* The change will increase product profitability, and finance will generally perceive this as the right thing to do	General communication on proposed changes to finance Modify finance systems to calculate new commission and claw back when sales do not conform

	Need to track order reject levels by salesperson, and overall customer order cancellation rate Claw-back on commission needs to be implemented				Develop revised management information sources, processes and system
10	Other members of the leadership team (excluding the sales director)	No significant impact, but may have to be able to describe change and rationale for change to staff and customers Need to provide resource to work on change initiative	Full understanding of the change, its implications and the underlying rationale	Significant other change work being driven by new corporate strategy following board review	*Positive/neutral*: the change will increase overall profitability, but this effect may be hidden amongst the effect of all the other ongoing projects across business	Develop executive presentation explaining changes and benefits Present in one to one sessions Update weekly management reports to include data on order reject rates Keep involved, try to ensure remain positive and keep their resources working on initiative

Table 5.5 **Sample list of change actions**

Step 5.6 Assess impact on infrastructure

So far in this chapter I have focused mainly on the human effects of change. As discussed in the introduction you also need to review what the impact of your change is on your infrastructure. This type of assessment relies on expertise and experience, and you should try to involve people who have been in your organisation for a long time and have experience of previous changes. These are the people who will say 'have you thought of ...?' If you have access to trained business analysts, they are often the best people to work with your experienced staff to assess the impact of the change on your infrastructure.

Here are some examples of infrastructure problems that have arisen on change projects I have been responsible for:

- Insufficient meeting room space in a proposed new building.
- Lack of adequate power supplies for new equipment which was to be installed in an office.
- Incompatibility between a new machine and existing machinery.
- Insufficient storage space after staff moved from permanent desks to hot desks.
- Poor quality of a roof on an existing warehouse that had been made the central warehouse for a business. The risk from the roof leaking when the warehouse was a minor storage area was limited, but when it became the main warehouse for the business with many millions of pounds of stock the risk was high.

It is true that for many changes it is likely that you will not foresee everything that will be affected by the change, and there will be some issues with your infrastructure post-change. However, that is not an excuse for not trying, the aim being to make your implementation as low risk and as painless as possible by planning all implications of the change.

There are three steps to identify the impact on your infrastructure:

- To determine what is affected by change, challenging any assumptions that the infrastructure will work as it does now after the change is implemented.
- To identify areas you do not understand and undertake a review of them.

- Based on this, to define the actions you need to undertake to ensure your infrastructure is adequate and will continue to work effectively following a change.

Step 5.7 Enhance change plan

The information you have gathered in Tables 5.4 and 5.5 provides a list of additional actions that must be added to the plan you developed in step 4 (plan how to achieve change).

Each of the actions should be built into the change plan, as for other tasks described in steps 4.3 and 4.4. Each action must be assigned an owner, ideally an individual within your change team, who is responsible for ensuring that this task is performed. This individual must have the skills, time and access to adequate resources to complete the action. As with all other tasks on the plan, these actions should have a set date for completion.

It is possible that some of the actions you have identified will already have been captured as part of the work you did to create your plan in the first place. That's fine. Reviewing capability and willingness to change is about ensuring the plan is complete, not necessarily adding hundreds of additional tasks.

Once you have done this, your change plan is sufficiently complete. Now it is time to move on to implementation.

Key tips

- To understand how an organisation will work once a change initiative is finished, change managers must assess and plan action from three perspectives:
  - Human response to change
  - Organisational readiness for change
  - Integration of change into existing infrastructure.
- You must determine the following for any change:
  - Who is affected by or can have an impact on the change?
  - What is the nature of this impact?

- What capability gaps do those groups have?
- What other changes are these groups also undergoing?
- What do you expect their response to the change to be?
- Do not forget to assess the impact on existing infrastructure.
- Based on this, update your change plan.

TO DO NOW

- Start to consider who will be affected by your change. What do you think their responses will be when they first hear about the change, and when the change is implemented?

- Consider if there are parts of your infrastructure that will be impacted by the change. How can you be sure – have you consulted widely with experienced members of your organisation who really understand how it all links together?

- Consider whether your change plan needs to be enhanced to take account of the actions you will take to manage responses and impact.

Step 6

Implement change

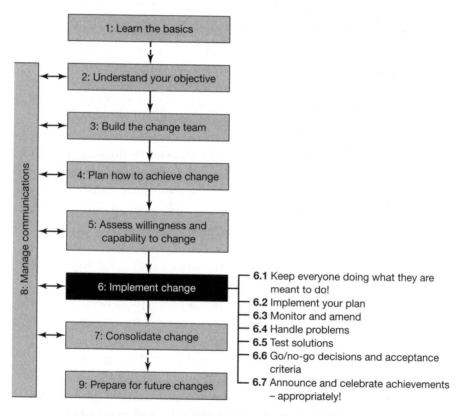

- 1: Learn the basics
- 2: Understand your objective
- 3: Build the change team
- 4: Plan how to achieve change
- 5: Assess willingness and capability to change
- 6: Implement change
- 7: Consolidate change
- 9: Prepare for future changes
- 8: Manage communications

6.1 Keep everyone doing what they are meant to do!
6.2 Implement your plan
6.3 Monitor and amend
6.4 Handle problems
6.5 Test solutions
6.6 Go/no-go decisions and acceptance criteria
6.7 Announce and celebrate achievements – appropriately!

THIS CHAPTER COVERS:

- Proceeding from an idea and a plan to an implemented change.

THE CENTRAL POINT IS:

- No matter how well you have completed the steps up to this point, it all counts for nothing until the change is implemented. Implementation is about making visions a reality, but implementation is also the time when your organisation is most exposed to risk from the change. Successful implementation is also about managing this risk.

Setting the scene

Consider the following four examples in which problems have occurred when implementing change:

1. A business decided it was time to upgrade its finance systems. The core financial systems were based on a standard suite of software from a major vendor, and had been significantly tailored over the years. This software was no longer supported by the vendor, and so the chief financial officer (CFO) decided it was time to upgrade to a newer version. As well as bringing the software up to date, the newer version had lots of new functionality and reporting capabilities that the finance team greatly valued. A consultancy was chosen to help implement the new software. The consultancy started work and asked for a lot of support from the finance staff in the organisation. The staff were needed to decide how precisely they wanted the software tailored and to design new business processes to use when the system was installed, as well as to support training and testing. The finance department was very supportive of the project as it could see the benefits and was excited about the opportunity. Unfortunately, the system would result in some of the administrative staff being no longer required and so they were less motivated than usual. Six months into the project the CFO performed a detailed review with the consultant project manager. The consultant presented progress and showed that the implementation was going very well. Given the importance of this project the CFO decided to report back to his peers on progress. He chose a meeting of the senior management team and told it all

about the project's progress, and how well the system was being implemented. He was expecting congratulations on a well-run project. He was surprised when a number of senior managers, including the operations, marketing and sales directors, instead of praising him, complained. The project was fine, but what about the day-to-day support they required from finance? Monthly reports were late, they did not know the status of key performance indicators, financial queries did not get answered, and they were not ready to start to develop next year's budget even though the deadline was looming.

2. The leadership team of an organisation decided that as a key part of preparing for the future it would implement a complete overhaul of the products it provided. The aim was to start implementing the new product set within six months. The marketing department was given responsibility for defining the new products that would be required and a plan of the next six months of work was defined. This showed all the steps to get to a position where the business had a complete set of new products defined. Work started, and some initial ideas were quickly generated. Unfortunately the fast start was not continued even though the marketing department was working very hard. A set of ideas for products was produced, and work would start on defining the products in detail. Then the product ideas were reviewed. Every time they were reviewed something was wrong, or more precisely it was felt something could be improved. In parallel with this, new ideas for products kept arising, partially from the creativity of the marketing staff, but also from observing what products competitors were releasing. After six months there was still very little agreement about what the new product set would consist of. Rather than implementing new products, this organisation was still designing them.

3. A nationwide organisation selling classified advertising performed a financial review and decided it was not making a large enough profit from certain types of advertising. The analysis was complex, because there were very many different types of adverts, and most customers bought a bundle of different adverts with various discounts and incentives. A new sales policy was introduced which was supported by some new products and a complete revision of the price list. The

policy and prices were explained to the sales force, who reluctantly accepted them, complaining of their complexity. Focus groups were run with customers, who generally responded well to the changes. The new prices were implemented nationwide. It did not take long for the results to come through – sales had plummeted.

4. A new customer relationship management system was developed by the IT department of a medium-sized business with about 2,500 employees. This system was a significant change for this business as it would enforce a much more structured way of managing customers than had previously been done. The system was fully developed, and having successfully completed technical testing the IT department felt it was ready for implementation. The decision to implement lay with the IT department. The new system was implemented over a weekend. When staff returned to work on Monday, there was chaos. Parts of the system did not work fully. Departments claimed they were not ready for it and did not know how to use it. Some teams had other changes being implemented on the same day and could not cope with so many changes at one time. The IT director was phoned by the COO (chief operating officer) and asked: how had the decision to implement been taken and who was involved in that decision? The COO made it very clear that she considered the project a failure.

Each of these examples shows what appear to be well-run change initiatives. However, in each case there are implementation problems. In the first example the finance department has become mesmerised by the project to implement a new finance system, and forgotten the need to continue to support the business on a day-to-day basis. This is a common problem on big projects, especially those sponsored by an active and senior executive like this CFO. It is true that to complete complex projects requires commitment, passion and focus, but there is a balance to be found, as this commitment, passion and focus cannot be at the expense of daily operations of the organisation.

The second example shows what happens if the change plan (as created in step 5) is not followed in implementation. Changes can always be perfected, but you have an end goal to achieve, and constantly tweaking and modifying change to bring it closer to perfection merely delays the point at which implementation starts. Obviously, you do not want to implement sub-standard ideas, but on the other hand, implementing an imperfect idea is better than implementing nothing at all. The second example shows one way in which a change project can get lost by not following the plan. Plans can always be revised if there really is a new idea that is radically better than what is being worked on, or a better approach to get to the desired end result, but forgetting the plan usually allows non-value-added tinkering. Normally new ideas add incremental benefit and only add a little to the length of a change, but the cumulative effect of many new ideas may mean the change initiative never finishes.

The third example shows how risk is involved in making change. No matter how much testing and customer input are taken for a change you cannot be absolutely certain how it will work in reality. Explaining the changes to staff and running customer focus groups reduced the risk from the change, but did not remove it altogether. A better answer may have been to trial the changes in one geographic region of the country before implementing them nationwide. In this way the change is tested for real, but on a small scale. Determining the risk mitigation approach for every change is an important part of the change manager's role and often requires specialist support from those familiar with risk assessment, tests, trials, pilots and contingency plans.

The final example shows the need to gain approval before implementing any change. An important part of all change projects must be to have a transparent process for agreeing when the change is ready for implementation with the most appropriate members of the organisation. To make this decision, previously agreed 'acceptance criteria' should be defined, and only if the change project meets these criteria should the implementation progress. In this case, leaving the decision to implement with the IT department and insufficient rigour in making that decision contributed to the failure of the project.

Introduction to implementing change

Implementation is the step where all change managers are eventually judged. The previous steps have all been about preparation, and it is critically important to use the time available to prepare for the smoothest possible implementation. However, nothing done in steps 1 to 5 is visible to more than a few people. Once a change is complete, no one will be remembered for a well-defined objective, a great change team, a fabulous plan or the best understanding of the organisation's willingness and capability to change. All of these things help towards success, but success or failure is only measured by how well a change is implemented.

Although implementation happens at the end of your change project, planning for implementation should start at the beginning of the initiative. A change project which does not adequately plan for implementation is unlikely to be successful. Planning is important in managing expectations and ensuring adequate time and resources are available for implementation, as some managers view implementation as easy and try to squeeze it into as short a time as possible. Implementation is the crunch time in your change. If you are late in any earlier part of your change, be late in implementation as well, rather than cut it short.

Implementation is about moving from a list of theoretical activities in a plan to doing these activities for real. There is not an absolute boundary between planning and implementation phases, as in reality a plan must adapt and be enhanced as a change initiative progresses, and also some implementation starts before the plan is complete. However, conceptually they are very different activities and most change projects move from a stage which is predominantly about thinking and preparing to one which is predominantly about doing.

No matter how much preparation has been done, a plan will never be a completely accurate representation of how a change project will actually turn out. There will be some activities that have been forgotten in planning, or take a longer or shorter time than was foreseen. Some activities will deliver the result expected, and some may deliver less or even prove to be irrelevant. A plan is like a map of a walk, essential else you will get lost, but looking at a map will never tell you exactly what every step of your journey is going to be like. The map gives you a route, and you can plan your route with great accuracy, but there will be unforeseen puddles to go round and obstacles to step over. No matter how good your map reading, if you can't go round the puddles and over the obstacles then you won't complete your walk.

As you go through your change initiative problems will occur; these should not lead to despair, but to creative searches for solutions. The best change managers are not those who plan so well that there are no problems, but the ones who do not get dismayed by problems, have built some degree of flexibility into a plan to provide time and resources to overcome problems, and who rapidly find efficient and effective solutions to them.

As a change progresses and becomes more visible to the whole organisation, staff will become more interested in the change. Sometimes they will be wary of the change, on other occasions they may positively welcome it and be excited by the potential it offers. Whichever response you get it is important to keep people focused on their normal jobs and not just the change project, as irrespective of how important your change is the organisation cannot stop operating whilst the change is being implemented. Keeping the organisation effectively productive whilst change is ongoing is a key element of successful implementation.

It is the nature of change management to expose your organisation to risk. No matter how fully you think you understand the change you are making, you cannot be absolutely certain that it will work flawlessly until it has been implemented. The implications of this depend on the nature of your change. When a minor change goes wrong it is normally nothing more than irritating, but complex and large-scale transformations can bankrupt or ruin an organisation if they fail. To minimise the risk to your organisation it is necessary to provide a way to test and trial changes until you are certain they can be implemented successfully. Planning for and executing relevant pilots, trials and tests is a crucial part of change implementation.

The step-by-step guide
STEP 6 – Implement change

Step 6.1 Keep everyone doing what they are meant to do!

In going through a change initiative an organisation is aiming to transition from an initial state to a new better state. This transition is not instantaneous, but happens through the life of a change project. The change project may take days, weeks, months or even years to complete, and during this time the organisation must continue to function and do whatever it normally does.

Change managers should never lose site of the fact that an organisation does not exist to implement change, but implements change to help it to continue to exist, survive and thrive. Whatever your organisation's objectives are, they are achieved through your normal day-to-day operations, (I use the term 'operations' in its broadest sense to mean all the standard activities your organisation does.) Therefore it is important to ensure that your change initiative minimises disruption to the current operations of the organisation. No one is going to thank the change manager for implementing a great change project if during the project no one does their normal work and the organisation loses all its customers.

In practice this means that during a change project everyone, apart from the change team, should keep doing their normal work at their expected level of performance until the change is complete.

It can be a major problem during change initiatives to keep staff concentrating on their day jobs. The awareness of change can cause concern, with worries about job security or the detrimental effects of change. Staff may have lower motivation and be distracted from work, they may spend time looking for new jobs, or in the worst cases can be deliberately disruptive. More positively, the awareness of change can bring excitement, especially if staff believe it will create an improved environment or a better organisation to work for. Such excitement can be very beneficial to the change initiative, but can also be unsettling to your normal operations. Excited people can take their eyes off the ball and spend their time talking and dreaming about the better future.

It is perfectly natural for everyone to respond to proposed change, but you must ensure that the response creates minimal interference to the normal operations of the organisation. This is helped by the way you plan the implementation, particularly:

- Being realistic about performance during change.
- Giving people a clear understanding of the direction and timing of the change.
- Applying good management control during the change.
- Providing appropriate incentives to continue working through the period of change.
- Controlling the disruption the change will bring about.

I discuss each of these in turn.

The starting point for change implementation is to be realistic about its impact on performance. Assuming you can run a large change initiative without disrupting performance is naïve. Unless you have great experience of implementing change in your organisation, it is difficult or impossible to scale this disruption, but expectations should be set that the organisation will not perform at peak performance throughout the life of the change initiative. If the change is managed well the drop in performance may be quite modest, but radical change will typically bring about major disruptions, I have seen over 50% drops in performance for short periods of time.

The leadership team should be used continually to explain what is happening. One of the key roles of leadership in change situations is continually to communicate a very clear direction of where the change is heading. There are some situations where it is necessary to keep change secret. However, even if change is unpopular, it is normally better to communicate an easily understandable image of what the change will bring. Even if this produces a negative response it is usually easier to manage this response than to manage the rumours and Chinese whispers that will occur when no direction is set and no communications are made. More positively, change may be perceived as beneficial by staff and communicating on change plans can be motivational.

There are a small number of people who really are perfectly happy working in chaotic situations without any view of what will happen tomorrow, but most people like to understand how their work will change in future. In modern organisations people do not typically expect an understanding of how the organisation will be in several years' time, but they certainly expect to have an understanding of how it will be over the next few months. Leaders at all levels in the organisation need constantly to give staff this picture through regular communications.

Use the line management hierarchy to support the change. Leadership is important, but in reality the main tool to keep people focused and performing in their normal jobs during a change situation is simply good day-to-day management discipline. If staff know what to expect, the line management community should be able to continue to motivate and focus them on their normal roles. As the change starts to be communicated to staff, managers should be briefed on the importance of keeping the organisation going. Staff should know that they will be measured by their normal performance measures. The organisation should be supportive and help people through the process of change, but that is not an excuse for poor performance. In simple terms this requires all managers to be told to keep doing the good jobs they normally do until they are told otherwise. This does need reinforcement, as managers themselves will be affected by thoughts of the change, and yet are critical to the ongoing functioning of the organisation during change. The best approach is normally openness and providing staff with an opportunity to share frankly any concerns. When staff know they have their manager's support, and know they can discuss any concerns they may have about change in a constructive dialogue, then the likelihood is that they will find it easier to concentrate on their normal work.

Occasionally it is appropriate to offer staff incentives to keep them working at their normal levels of performance during a change. This should be the exception. Staff in a modern organisation should expect change as part of any job, and should not anticipate additional rewards simply for going through change. However, there are some situations in which it is overly idealistic to expect full attention on work. For example, it is unrealistic to assume that people will work hard and deliver a full output when they have been told that they will be made redundant. In these extreme cases, and where roles are critical to the functioning of the organisation, incentives need to be found to keep people working hard until they leave the organisation. Payment of performance and retention bonuses, helping staff to find new jobs and offering other financial incentives may be required. However, often, simple things like greater flexibility in working hours and regularly thanking people for continuing effort can help tremendously.

Critically, to keep the organisation operational during change, disruption should be planned for. Disruption will occur. Some staff will be allocated to the change project, so will not perform their normal role. Other staff will often have to be taken temporarily out of their normal roles to go through education and training. Even with good training, when change is implemented people will be unfamiliar with working in a new way and are likely to have lower performance until they develop experience. The following points are important when planning for disruption:

- *Timing*: implement change at the time when the impact is least for the organisation, especially if during implementation normal services cannot be provided. Implementing change at Christmas or during the January sales in shops is normally foolhardy. Altering systems and processes at the start of the academic year is probably not ideal in universities and schools. Ensuring the timing of change is appropriate is largely about understanding the peaks and troughs in the workload of your organisation, what other events and changes are occurring, and applying a little common sense.

- *Staffing levels*: as the change progresses more and more staff time will be needed for activities such as communications and awareness, feedback sessions, training and education, and testing. Each of these activities has an impact on the available resources, and reduces the capability to complete the organisation's normal workload. This can be overcome partially by timing and the use of overtime, but you may also need to bring in temporary additional staff. The costs of overtime and temporary staff should be built into the budget for the change. Temporary staff may need training in the roles they will perform whilst the normal job owners are working on the change. A plan which includes recruitment and training time for temporary staff can show it is necessary to bring in temporary staff some months in advance of the time they are actually needed to do the job for real.

- *Performance expectations*: set expectations of decreases in performance when staff are unavailable for normal work, and shortly after being told about unpopular changes. Keep stressing to management the need for them to drive performance during implementation. If there is a particular time when the organisation's service will decline as you implement the change, warn your customers. They may not like it, but they will almost certainly prefer being warned and having the option of planning alternatives than finding out that you cannot serve them when they are desperate for something you provide.

Step 6.2 Implement your plan

Now the preparation is over and it is time to implement your plan. This step is where the bulk of your change initiative occurs, yet it is one of the shortest in the book. This is because it is about following your plan, which is unique to your situation. You have done all the preparation you can do, so now find the first activity on the plan and start it!

Depending on the nature of your change your plan may be anything from a very precise schedule of activities, such as might be typical in a software development project or the development and launch of a new product, to a looser timeline of key events and milestones, such as might be typical of a cultural change programme. Either way, now is the time to start working through the activities on the plan to achieve your end objective.

Whilst stating bluntly that to complete work you must start it seems unnecessarily obvious, organisations can spend huge amounts of time deciding to start, then asking for revisions to plans, and even asking for rethinking of what is being done. It is usually better to start an imperfect project than constantly delay work in the hope of better ideas appearing.

Typically the responsibility for managing progress to plan falls to the change manager. For a larger change the change manager may have a dedicated project manager as part of the change team.

Most change projects do not have a fixed point when planning has finished and implementation has started, but there is normally an obvious time when you are moving from predominantly thinking and planning to predominantly doing and delivering. When you reach this time ensure that all the members of the change team understand that the project is moving into implementation. Where appropriate, the wider organisation affected by the change must also know that implementation has started.

Step 6.3 Monitor and amend

Activities do not often occur spontaneously, tasks must be managed to happen in the right way at the right time. A change initiative is no different, and to ensure it proceeds correctly towards the objective, progress must be managed.

To manage activity, you must have an understanding of progress towards the objective of that activity. This is achieved by monitoring the tasks you have done and will be doing. Monitoring progress in a change situation requires consideration of two separate dimensions of progress:

- *Progress relative to the plan*: are you completing the tasks you expected to complete in the timeline you originally defined and within the costs you originally expected?

- *Progress relative to achieving the objective*: as you complete the activities in your plan, are they bringing about change which is resulting in the expected benefit to your organisation? (This benefit is measured in terms of the primary measure you defined in step 2.4 of this book.)

In simple terms you need to know what has been done, what has been achieved, how long it took and how much it cost.

The most important dimension of progress for a change manager is progress relative to objectives, as in the end it does not matter whether you have completed certain tasks or not, but it does matter if you have achieved your objective or not. This should not be forgotten, as there can be a tendency to assume success because tasks are being completed. It seems too obvious to state that success is only achieved if the desired outcome is achieved, but many managers lose sight of this and happily go on completing tasks irrespective of the outcome.

That does not mean that you can ignore the completion of tasks in the plan. It is crucially important to measure progress relative to the plan as well. Experience shows that unless this is done, change initiatives will drag on and take an extended period of time. You want not only to achieve your objective, but to achieve it within the time defined in your plan and for the cost you expected.

If you find it is taking longer or costing more, you may need to revisit your approach. Measuring progress gives you the signal when to rethink your approach. Additionally, you must measure progress relative to the plan because this provides you with the information to guide and direct the change team on a day-to-day basis. When tasks are completed the next set needs to be allocated to the change team. Where tasks are not being completed in time you must find out how to help the responsible member of the change team to complete them.

Progress to plan should be measured continuously. This will happen informally all the time as your work progresses, but typically needs to be supported by formal progress review meetings. The frequency of these meetings depends on the nature of the change, but once a week will help to maintain good progress.

The basic process for monitoring and managing progress to plan is the work of a project manager. A project manager does many things, but central to his or her role is looking at what tasks are completed, comparing these to what should have been completed, and then asking questions of the type:

- Is the project on schedule, relative to the plan? (Have you done less, more or exactly what was expected?)
- Are there any trends to be worried about?
- If there is any slippage – what is its impact? Can this slippage be caught up or does some action need to be taken to bring you back in line with the plan?

Progress relative to the objective you have set out can be harder to assess continually, and typically is measured at defined periodic intervals. The length of these intervals is dependent on the objective. If you are making a change which should increase sales in a chain of shops, with good systems you may be able to measure progress towards the objective daily or weekly. On the other hand, if your change is to improve staff satisfaction, you may be able to measure this monthly, but probably for practical reasons it will be over even longer periods of time.

It can be difficult to present an overall view of progress both relative to tasks and relative to achieving your objectives. One good way to show these two dimensions to progress is on a simple grid as shown in Figure 6.1. The vertical dimension of the grid represents progress relative to the plan and completion of activity. The higher up the scale, the faster you are progressing relative to the plan. The horizontal dimension of the grid represents progress relative to hitting objectives and delivering benefits. The further to the left, the more benefits are being achieved. The ideal position is in the top left-hand corner: more benefits delivered than expected and faster than expected. The expected position is in the middle. The worst position is in the bottom right-hand corner: fewer benefits delivered than expected and slower than expected.

The figure represents an example of a change programme made up of seven initiatives. By looking at this grid you can quickly see how well each initiative is going. For example, you can conclude that initiative 1 is in trouble as it is both late (in other words, fewer activities have been done that were planned to be done by this time) and underachieved (in other

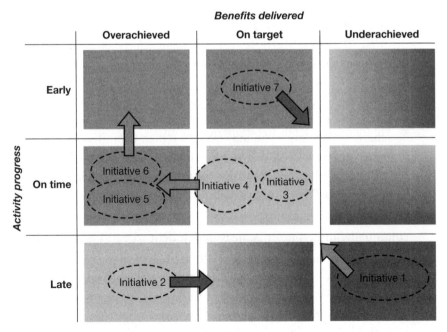

Figure 6.1 Graphic representation of change initiative status

words, the activities completed have delivered less benefit than expected). On the other hand, initiative 6 is in a good position as it is on time (in other words, what was expected to be done has been done) and overachieved (in other words, the tasks completed have delivered more benefit than was expected). By adding directional arrows you can also show the trend in progress, so although initiative 1 is in trouble, it is improving, whereas initiative 7 is getting worse. By using such a simple diagram a lot of information is provided and it can be used to communicate progress to a wide audience.

The purpose of monitoring is of course not only to understand the status of your change initiative, but also to enable you to take management action. The actions you take will be dependent on the situation, but in essence fall into one of the following categories:

- *If the change is late*: take action to speed up progress. Such action can be as simple as pushing the change team to work harder, but this will only work if the amount of time to catch up is fairly small. Beyond this you may have to look at other ways to complete tasks faster. You may use some of the contingency time built into your plan. You may be able to remove some of the less important tasks from your plan. You may also need to consider adding more people to the change team.

- *If the change is not meeting objectives/benefits*: take action to increase the level of objectives achieved. Typically, if you are not achieving objectives, you will have to modify your approach. If the gap between what you are achieving and what you expected to achieve is very large, you may need to replan the initiative, adding extra tasks which will deliver more benefit. One trap to avoid is just to hope for more benefit whilst the project continually delivers less than expected. If your plan does not deliver the benefits you need, change it.

What if everything is happening as expected and you are on time and delivering the benefits expected? Good change managers do not wait until progress is late or objectives are underachieved before taking action. If you really are completely on track it is time to ask yourself if you can go faster, deliver more, or release some resources from the change project.

Step 6.4 Handle problems

As you progress through your change initiative, sometimes things will go wrong. There will be setbacks and problems will occur. The ability to handle problems well differentiates those managers who are really excellent at driving change from those who merely dabble.

In any project situation problems will arise that were unforeseen at the start, and which need to be resolved before the project can be completed. Project managers call such problems 'issues' and the process for managing them 'issue management'. Good preparation and planning will avert many difficulties, but it will never avoid all of them. This is especially true when the project you are involved in is a change initiative.

Some changes can seem amorphous, and planning and preparation may give more of a sense of direction than a full and detailed set of step-by-step instructions, so it is often inherent in change plans that there will be a need to react to unplanned occurrences. Changes deal with people, and people will react at times in unexpected and unforeseen ways. Change affects organisations and organisations are highly complex and difficult to predict fully. The problems that arise will be very varied: for example, what you saw as only a great beneficial change will be perceived as a threat and will generate a negative response which you must spend time overcoming; at some crucial point in time someone will not do what they were meant to; a part of your infrastructure will not work in the way you expected when you make a change; someone in the change team will interpret what you thought were clear instructions in an unforeseen way; a core task will take twice as long as you planned.

If you do not resolve problems promptly and effectively then you risk delaying or even stopping your change. Irrespective of the nature of the problem, there are five actions that will enable you to manage them well:

- *Start by expecting problems and build contingency into your plan*: your capability to solve problems starts with the plan you built in step 5. Solving problems requires you to have the time and resource to develop solutions. If you have built your plan with no contingency, then every time something unexpected happens your initiative will simply become delayed or cost more than the plan states. It is true that some activities will take less time than expected, but it is very rare that the benefits of quicker and cheaper tasks balance with those that take longer or cost more than planned. Unless there is some contingency in terms of a buffer of time and resources, then you will have no capacity to solve unforeseen issues. The amount of contingency you need is dependent on the level of risk and familiarity in your change project, as well as how important it is that you complete the work in the expected time and for the expected budget. Where the initiative is of a very familiar type of change, and when you are not worried if it takes a bit longer or costs more than planned, then you need low levels of contingency. Where it is a completely unknown and new type of change, and where you must complete it in your defined timescales and for the agreed budget, you need more contingency. Determining the amount of contingency required in a plan is the skill of a professional project manager. Don't fall into the trap of thinking that contingency is not required. Contingency shows an understanding that real life is not fully predictable.

- *Be alert and listen*: a core requirement for anyone managing any type of change initiative is to be alert, constantly observing and listening to the team and the organisation as a whole. You may by pure chance be the first person to observe a problem, but usually you have to rely on others to tell you about it. It is best to know about problems as early as possible, and to do this you need to be consciously alert for them. By understanding problems early you have the most time to resolve them, and often a problem attacked early is simple to resolve. Encourage openness and discussion, otherwise you will find you only know about problems when the initiative has failed. (In project management there is the concept of risk management. Risk management is all about identifying problems *before* they occur and taking action to reduce the impact they have on the initiative or the likelihood of them occurring.)

- *Define and document the problem*: knowing that there is a problem is not the same as knowing what the problem really is. When you know you have a problem don't just jump to solutions. Spend a little time making sure you really understand what the problem is. This requires searching for its root causes, not simply reacting to the immediately observable symptoms. Always document your problems. This is important for two reasons. Firstly, in any complex change you will have lots of problems arising as you work. If you do not document them they have a habit of being forgotten, and only being found again when they have stopped all progress. Secondly, forcing yourself to write down a problem in a concise form of words is a good test to see if you really understand it.

- *Assess and determine counteraction*: Once you have a real understanding you must determine some counteraction either to solve the problem (this is best) or, if that is really not possible, to overcome any impact the problem has. (To understand the difference consider a problem you could have: your change project is running over budget. To solve this you need more money; however, if this is not possible you can reduce the impact of this problem by trying to complete the project for less.) Sometimes the solutions to problems are obvious, and clarity in defining your problem will greatly speed up the identification of the best solution. On other occasions the solution is less clear and you may need to get other people's advice or run a brainstorming session to look for solutions. With discussion you will often find that even quite complex problems have clear solutions if you invite other people's ideas.

- *Take your action and assess result*: your counteraction will hopefully solve your problem, but do not assume this. Always check the result and make sure it has really solved your problem and not merely hidden it from view!

Occasionally, even with the best plans and the fullest use of contingency, something occurs that really does mean you cannot complete the work within the original timelines or budget. Before accepting this, it is worth bringing together a team to review the plan and the problem and determine whether any creative or novel solutions can be found. However, if this is not possible you really have no choice but to replan your initiative. In some cases this will require going back through steps 5.4 to 5.6.

It is often not a single problem that causes your change initiative to go beyond of your plan, but the cumulative impact of many problems. This will never be seen by looking at a problem and its impact in isolation, but can only be identified by understanding your trends in progress. This is very important for change initiatives, as they are quite likely to throw up many small problems, often relating to individuals or small groups of people. In isolation you can solve each problem within the plan, but the cumulative impact can take you beyond your expected plan. Many change projects have unwittingly been found to be significantly late and overspent because of an unobserved trend of small slippages and expenditures that were not planned for.

Step 6.5 Test solutions

As your change project progresses you will reach a point when you want to implement the whole or a part of your change for real. This is often the riskiest stage of your change. There are two steps to help reduce this risk – checking that your solution to change works properly, which is done by testing, and making a formal decision to accept the change, which is dealt with below.

Before you implement any solution you want to have a high level of certainty that it works as you wanted and does not cause any problems for your organisation. Testing is a key way to reduce this type of risk. The way testing is done is quite specific to the type of change you are making. You will test a new IT system differently from new marketing materials, and a refurnished office differently from a modified set of procedures. However, whatever the nature of the change, you cannot be certain that any solution you have designed will actually work until you try it. Testing reduces risk by providing a way to try some or all of your solution in a controlled way before implementation across the whole organisation. Testing is also one of the main sources of information for acceptance or rejection of change in step 6.6.

There are three components to testing:

- *Formal tests*: testing is the formal and structured process of ensuring that a change works before you implement it into the live operations of your business. For engineers and software developers, testing is a specialist discipline in its own right. There can be several stages of testing – typically starting by testing individual components and gradually pulling all components together until you can do a 'systems test' or an 'integration test'. Following this, a new system is tested by the users who defined the original requirements to ensure it works as expected; this is normally called a 'user acceptance test' or UAT. Finally there may be an operational test where the system is integrated with the complete infrastructure of an organisation to ensure it works. Only then can it go live. Good tests require planning and the development of test scripts. Test scripts define what is to be tested and the expected outcome from a test. A test team is normally responsible for running the test scripts. Where testing is to be done, it should be planned by someone with experience of designing and running tests. Testing is a key way of reducing implementation risk, and for some changes, especially those depending on technical developments, it is normally regarded as a mandatory phase of any change project. A common acceptance criterion is normally for a minimum level of tests to have been passed, typically 90% or more.

- *Internal pilots*: internal pilots are the implementation of a change in a limited part of an organisation. Having tested a change, one way to implement it is the 'big bang' approach. That is, literally making the same change across your organisation at once. Unfortunately, some changes cannot easily be tested in conjunction with the infrastructure or operations prior to implementation, and even if you have rigorously tested the change there is still a residual risk that it will not work without causing disruption. The way to avoid the risk associated with a big bang implementation is to implement your change for real, but in a limited part of the organisation. This is called a pilot implementation. So, you may just implement the change in one department or one geographic area of your organisation. Before you roll out the change across the whole organisation you run the pilot for some time, observe and collect results on the outcome, and where necessary tweak the change. Piloting is a very useful way of reducing risk.

- *Customer trials*: a customer trial is where a customer-affecting change is implemented for a limited group of customers before being implemented for all customers. Customer trials are most common for new products and services, but can also be used for any customer visible change such as a new order form. Any time the change you are making affects the products or services you supply to your customers, you should consider running a customer trial. If you are a B2B business you may select a small group of customers; for a B2C business you may for example try the change in a limited geographic region. Trialling customers enables you to understand the full customer response more completely than techniques such as market research and focus groups ever will. It also enables you to check how well the change works in the real world as opposed to in a plan.

Testing, piloting and trialling are essential parts of many change initiatives. They reduce risk significantly, but of course at a cost. Tests, trials and pilots take time, and use resources – often requiring specialised and sometimes expensive support. There are different ways to design tests, some of which can be faster and more effective than others. Generally, though, the longer and more extensive the testing, the lower the risk, but at the cost of a longer and more expensive project and a longer time to wait until you start to receive the benefits from the project. There is always a tension point between the amount of testing, trialling and piloting done against the cost and the time to finish, and the need to avoid risk and negative impact on the organisation. Good tests, trials and pilots for complex or radical developments may take up a very significant proportion of the time on a change initiative – sometimes even more than half the length of the whole initiative. Whilst it is theoretically possible to do too much testing, cutting it short does expose you to risk. To shorten the length of testing, some test stages can be done in parallel, but in the end it is a choice between the risk you want to take and the speed and cost of implementation.

By running tests, trials and pilots you will be hoping that they prove that the change you are undertaking works well. However, if nothing ever went wrong then there would be no point in tests. The outcome from any form of testing, trialling and piloting may theoretically show that the change is 100% perfect, but in practice it will always throw up some problems with your change. Therefore you must be prepared to make modifications to your proposed change as a result of these activities. Some problems will have to be fixed before you go live, but if you understand the risk it is legitimate to decide to fix others after going live. However, anything left to be fixed after then should be minor. Many organisations have the habit of planning to fix problems after going live, only to find higher priority projects to start, and such problems never get fixed.

Step 6.6 Go/no-go decisions and acceptance criteria

Step 6.6 is only relevant to some types of change. To understand if it is relevant to your specific change, consider two examples of very different types of change initiatives:

- *Initiative 1 is a change based on an IT enhancement*: the initiative aims to improve productivity by replacing some old software with new enhanced software. Firstly, the new software must be developed. As with a normal software development project there will be a period of collecting requirements, followed by development of the software, which will then be tested. Once the software has been tested it will be ready to 'go live' – that is, being used in real life to support the day-to-day operations of the organisation. In this situation there is a very clear boundary when the organisation moves from its current state (using the old software) to a new state (working with the new software). Staff may go home on Friday evening having worked with the old software, the new software is installed and goes live at the weekend, and the staff return on Monday morning to work with the new version.

- *Initiative 2 is a change to deliver a new organisational culture*: such a change programme can take a significant amount of work, but there is no single point in time when the new culture goes live. You can never truly identify a boundary and say today the organisation has one culture and tomorrow it will have a different one. The creation of a new organisational culture takes time and will gradually percolate through the staff and management. It may be supported by specific timed events such as staff communication sessions and the implementation of a new performance management system, but the whole change initiative is about the gradual migration from an existing to a new state.

This step deals with the process of taking changes from a development stage into the live operations of your organisation. As such it is only really applicable to those changes that have a clear point of transition from the old to the new state, such as the first example above. In changes like the second example specific activities may have clear points of implementation, but the overall change has no one point to go live.

The first reason why there needs to be a process for managing the transition between development and going live is that no matter how well you have planned your change, there is always a risk it will not work. Organisations, and their component parts, are highly complex combinations of people, processes, IT systems and infrastructure. Good planning and a well-run project will significantly reduce risk to your organisation, but there will always remain a residual risk of an unpredicted outcome which is detrimental to your organisation. The second reason for having a formal decision point between development and going live is to ensure that when a decision is made to go live it is made because the solution is ready, and not because of management pressure. There can be intense pressure to implement change to gain the benefits or simply to finish a project. Unless the solution is ready for implementation, going live will cause more trouble than it is worth. Making the decision explicit reduces the ability for any one manager to force a change into live operations for which it was not yet ready.

The criticality of the unpredicted outcome from change is related to how much risk is associated with the change. A change to a minor procedure used by a back office function will usually represent a low risk to your organisation, and can probably be implemented without too much concern – you can bear the risk of the change going wrong. If the change does go wrong, a further modification can be made to the now live procedure without significant problems arising. However, not all changes are like this. Some changes, if they go wrong, pose significant risk to the day-to-day operations of your organisation and even to its ongoing existence. For example, if you change the software that runs the tills in a chain of shops and it does not work properly when the shops open, then you cannot take your customers' money and you have a major problem which if not resolved rapidly could bankrupt the business.

So what can you do about this type of risk? The solution to minimising risk has several stages. The first stage is to spend time designing your change well. The better designed your change, the lower the risk of its going wrong. Also, it is far, far easier and cheaper to fix mistakes when you are designing a change than when it is being implemented. However, organisations, the staff in them, the working processes, IT systems and other infrastructure are immensely complicated and it is often impractical to try to assess every single possible response to change. Great design alone is not a foolproof way to remove risk when going live and ensure that when you make a change nothing will go wrong which disrupts your organisation: a new IT system may have a bug in it, a new procedure may not work in some unforeseen circumstances, some responsibility may be forgotten when an organisation is reorganised. There is almost an infinite variety of things that can go wrong.

There are four stages that will reduce risk from implementing change. These are:

- *Assessing the risk to your organisation from a change*: to make an assessment of the impact on your organisation if the change goes wrong. What will happen if the change does not work when you implement it? What is the likelihood that it will not work?

- *Defining acceptance criteria*: having some clear predefined criteria for deciding whether the change initiative has developed a solution that is of sufficiently low risk to your organisation. Acceptance criteria ensure that the quality of work done on a change project is measured in some agreed way and the change is implemented only if it meets the necessary level of quality.

- *Having a go/no-go decision*: an agreed point in the change project, when an appropriate group of people come together to decide, using the acceptance criteria, whether to implement the change or not.

- *Building a supporting contingency plan for going live*: to have a plan that can be activated should something go wrong once the change has been implemented.

I describe each of these briefly.

Assessing the risk to your organisation from a change helps to determine the amount of effort you should put into risk reduction exercises. If the risk is low then the relative amount of effort you will want to spend on reducing risk is small. If the risk is high then the relative amount of effort you spend on reducing risk is high. For highly risky projects a very significant proportion, and occasionally even the majority, of the overall time can be spent on activities such as testing and trialling. (As an extreme example, consider changes to a nuclear power plant – the risk of a mistake is often low, but the implications of a mistake can be huge, hence vast amounts of time and effort spent ensuring that any change is risk free.)

Understanding the risk you are taking is also important in terms of gaining approval for a change. In step 5 you gained approval for your change based on the business case looking at the comparison of costs and benefits, but no matter how good the business case is, if the risk of a change is very high your leadership team may choose not to do it.

How you assess risk requires judgement and experience of the type of change being implemented and your specific organisation. You need to consider the likelihood of change going wrong, which needs to consider factors such as the complexity, novelty, scale and speed of change as well as the skill and experience of your change team. You also need to consider the impact if the change does go wrong. Will it have a minor impact or will it cripple your organisation?

Once you understand the risk, you need to determine how you will assess whether your specific change initiative is in a suitable state to go live. The information you need to make this decision is called 'acceptance criteria'. Acceptance criteria are predefined and measurable parameters. Acceptance criteria should be defined by the change team, and approved by the managers of the areas affected by the change. The sources of acceptance criteria can be many and varied, but typical sources include technical tests, pilots and customer trials (these were discussed in more detail in Step 6.5). So, an acceptance criterion for new software may be that the software has no major bugs, and fewer than 10 minor bugs. You may also make assessments of business readiness for a change; for example, the percentage of staff who have been trained for a change, with an acceptance criterion that at least 95% must be trained before the change can be implemented. Another acceptance criterion may be that a solution has to meet 100% of the mandatory requirements and at least 80% of the optional requirements. Yet another acceptance criterion may be that specific managers in operational departments affected by the change have all formally agreed that they are willing to accept the change.

Go/no-go decisions are key milestones in the life of your change programme. A go/no-go decision is an explicit decision to progress or stop a change initiative based on your acceptance criteria. The most important go/no-go decision is just prior to going live, but for major change programmes there may be several decisions between different stages of the programme.

The decision makers for a go/no-go decision should be the key stakeholders who will be affected by a change when it goes live. The change team should advise them of the status of the change and their opinion of whether it is in a state to go live, but it is an important part of change management that whoever is being changed needs to accept the change. They will accept the change if the acceptance criteria they think are important have been met.

Although a go/no-go decision should be based on your defined acceptance criteria it is often not an absolutely clear-cut decision and requires a degree of management judgement.

The final stage of risk management is to have some contingency plans when going live. These consist of rapidly executable plans, backed by access to adequate resources, that can be triggered should events after a change not be as you required. Again it is not possible to define a generic contingency plan, but typical components might include a way to rescind the change and roll back to the state prior to the change being implemented. Less dramatically, a contingency plan may incorporate a support team on call which can rapidly assist any areas of your organisation in difficulty once the change is implemented.

Step 6.7 Announce and celebrate achievements – appropriately!

There is nothing like the perception of success to help to motivate teams, and change teams are no different. When a change initiative starts to be successful and is delivering benefits to your organisation, this should be communicated, and where appropriate celebrated.

Celebration is an excellent way to motivate teams. It gives people an opportunity to relax from what can be quite high pressure on a big change initiative. Celebration is a good advert for the change initiative. When success becomes visible it will tend to become easier to find people who actively want to work on the change initiative, and you will find opponents rapidly becoming supporters as success is announced. If you are going to celebrate, do it properly and in a way that the change teams enjoy and value.

However, only celebrate when you really have something to celebrate, and when it is a good time for everyone to have a short break from the hard work. Announcing success but having later to say you were wrong will damage your change initiative. Having disproportionate celebrations for minor achievements risks developing cynicism, and can develop unrealistic expectations as to what will happen when you really do deliver a big change.

There is an additional risk that if you celebrate too early people can stop focusing on driving progress, thinking that the work is over. Achievement of a noteworthy success should not be confused with a change initiative being complete, and in celebrating you should be sure that everyone knows you may be taking a well-deserved breather, but tomorrow it is back to work as usual.

Key tips

- An organisation does not exist to implement change, but implements change to help it to continue to exist, survive and thrive. When change is underway, make sure that the organisation continues to do all the normal work that needs to be done in priority to the change itself.
- Nothing is ever delivered if implementation is not started – and completed!
- Monitor progress in terms of both completion of tasks and the delivery of benefits.
- Monitor progress in terms of both progress at any one point in time as well as the trend over time.
- Expect problems and resolve them quickly and effectively.
- The decision to go live requires an understanding of the risk being taken. Risk can be minimised by activities like testing and contingency plans, but there is never zero risk.
- Celebrate success proportionately and at the right time.

TO DO NOW

- Start communicating with your line management and prepare them for the change that is coming, but also tell them that it is business as usual for their departments whilst the change project progresses.

- Decide if you need the support of a professional project manager on your team.

- Make sure you have fully planned your approach to managing the risk of implementing your change.

- Stop prevaricating and looking for perfect approaches – start implementing your plan!

Step 7

Consolidate change

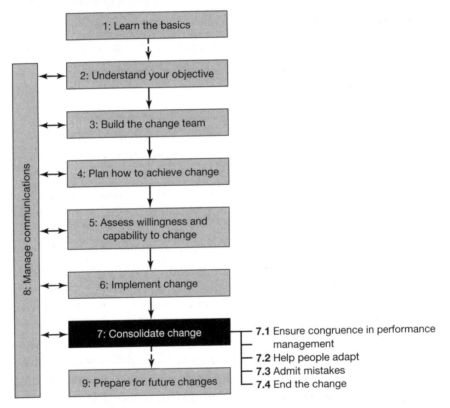

1: Learn the basics

2: Understand your objective

3: Build the change team

4: Plan how to achieve change

5: Assess willingness and capability to change

6: Implement change

7: Consolidate change

8: Manage communications

9: Prepare for future changes

7.1 Ensure congruence in performance management
7.2 Help people adapt
7.3 Admit mistakes
7.4 End the change

THIS CHAPTER COVERS:

- Techniques to help sustain change.

> ## THE CENTRAL POINT IS:
>
> - The benefits of change are rarely delivered in one instant, but accrue over a period of time. Change can be fragile; organisations can often revert back to old ways of working and achievements may not be maintained. Avoiding this requires active support beyond the point of implementation to consolidate the change and ensure benefits are sustained.

Setting the scene

Consider the following examples of post-implementation events, which each show different ways in which change can unravel even though implementation was complete:

1. The leadership team in an organisation was performing a review and realised that one of the main blockages to higher performance was the tendency for people to work in their functional silos, not to think about processes on an end-to-end basis, but to strive to achieve their own local objectives often at the expense of overall organisational objectives. A cultural change programme was started, with an emphasis on developing team work across functional boundaries. There was a lot of support and positive energy for this programme and it was progressing well. Cross-functional teams were brought together, and long-standing interdepartmental problems were resolved. Relationships across the organisation were improved, and what once would have caused angry words and simmering resentment between departments was now settled with a quick phone call or a friendly meeting. Many different departments were involved in this change programme, but one area that did not engage in this change programme was the service delivery department. The head of service delivery continued to achieve great performance in his area, but generally with complete disregard for the impact on other functions. It was therefore noted with some irritation by the staff when the head of service delivery received a large bonus and was promoted to a Director. Although the organisation was trying to move away from working in functional

silos, here a senior manager had been rewarded for demonstrating precisely the behaviour the organisation did not want. Not surprisingly this had a negative impact on the cultural change programme, and staff started to develop very cynical views about it.

2. A business had great revenues, but the profit margin was lower than many of its competitors, and significantly lower than the most profitable company in the sector. A root cause was identified to be the business's customer base. The customers tended to be poorer and much more price sensitive than those of the competitors. Additionally, rates of bad debt were high. The sales force was commissioned on revenues and was very successful at continually increasing total revenues, thus of course increasing their commission payments. The main advantage of the current customers was that there were lots of them, giving the opportunity for high total sales and revenues. The company decided to start to push into more profitable customer groups. Although there were fewer such customers, and revenues could drop, it was still expected that overall profitability would increase as prices could be raised. The marketing department spent a lot of time analysing and profiling customers, and developing new sales collateral to enable these customers to be targeted and successfully sold to. The sales force was extensively trained in how to identify, approach and sell to the new customer base. A few months later it was recognised that little had changed. Sales was still selling to a very similar customer group as originally, and it was realised that the sales commission had not been modified as part of the change.

3. A charismatic new boss was brought in to run a division of a public services organisation. The new boss was keen to shake up the organisation and to make her mark. She felt that performance could be dramatically improved with investments in new technology. Initially her senior management team was supportive, trusting her judgement and experience. Several investments were made and many staff ended up with much better PCs and various mobile devices. It did create a lot of good feeling towards the new boss, and when she went around the organisation she received much positive feedback from staff who felt they were receiving investment and attention. This did have an impact and performance improved.

However, some of the senior managers realised that this good feeling would be short lived and could not really understand how the investment would actually improve performance in the longer term. In fact they knew the investment was really a mistake and money would be better used elsewhere. There were certainly cheaper ways to excite and motivate staff. But no one was going to tell the boss who had just come up with yet another set of technology enhancements to make.

These three examples show that change can go wrong after it has been implemented, undermining the achievement of desired objectives. In the first example, a great change programme is spoilt by the inconsistent behaviour of one senior manager; worse than his behaviour is the impression that he has actually been rewarded for behaving in this way. One event may not really undermine a change programme, but senior managers repeatedly behaving in conflict with the change principles will. The second example is about performance management. In this case the primary management lever to motivate sales staff, the commission payment system, is effectively encouraging them to ignore a desired change completely. The commission system should been aligned with the change, for example by commissioning on profit margin not revenues. The third example shows how even the best intentioned change can be a mistake, in which case it is better to identify the mistake quickly, and modify the approach. Covering up mistakes is always an error.

Introduction to consolidating change

There is rarely an obvious boundary point at which a change can be said to be fully implemented. A change project may be over, but that does not mean the process of change is complete. Even when all the components of the change have been implemented, change can come undone. Successful change requires adapting the way people work and behave, their skills and capabilities, and even the ways they think and their attitudes. But people always have a choice, and no matter how much effort and time you put into your change, staff may choose not to work or behave in the way you want. After implementation you have to consolidate change, so it gets to a point where the change is no longer even considered as new, but is regarded as the normal way of working.

Key to ensuring that change does not unravel is your performance management approach. Modifying the way you manage, motivate and encourage great performance in your staff is an important part of many changes, and can even be the core component of a change. Without bringing your performance management in line with your change, you risk sending conflicting signals to your staff. What are members of staff to do if a change project tells them to behave in one way, and yet the way they are performance managed encourages them to behave in a contrary fashion? Many staff will end up listening to messages from your performance management approach, especially if it directly affects their remuneration and other rewards.

Just because you and some other people are ready for change, and have accepted the change, does not mean that all your staff have. There is often a macho style of change management which behind all the soft messages is really saying 'accept the change or leave the organisation'. In the end some people may have to leave the organisation, but it is unreasonable to expect staff to accept change automatically just because you say it is good. Additionally, you do not want to lose good staff simply because you have not put in enough effort to explain the rationale for change and given people long enough to adapt to it. The need for managers to help and convince staff to accept change will often have to go on for some time after the change has been implemented. In fact, you can argue that one of the key roles of managers in a modern organisation is to help staff to adapt continuously to incessant changes.

Risk is inherent in change, and to overcome this you need to be alert to the situations in which change really does not work, and rapidly take action to make subsequent modifications to overcome the problems change will sometimes create. The willingness to admit mistakes and make revisions can be daunting in some organisational cultures, but unless there is an ability to admit frankly when things have gone wrong, you actually increase rather than decrease risk.

The step-by-step guide
STEP 7 – Consolidate change

Step 7.1 Ensure congruence in performance management

A key component of many changes is for staff to work or behave in a different way. People always have a choice about how they work, and unless there is some reason to adapt the way they work, they will not necessarily do it. Management dictum alone will not achieve 100% conformance to a change. Therefore, whenever you attempt to change what your staff do or the way that they do it, you must also change how you measure and motivate them. Put another way, your performance management approach must be congruent with your objectives. On many occasions I have seen great change programmes fail because the organisation involved continued to use an old performance management framework that did not encourage acceptance of the change, or, even worse, actively discouraged its uptake. The second example at the start of this chapter is a classic case in point, and lots of changes to sales and marketing have failed because of a lack of consistency between the desired objective and the key performance lever for sales – commission payments. The sales force is not only being rational, but following delivery of the performance your process actually encourages.

In the context of this book I use the term 'performance management' to include both formal and informal performance management. The formal performance management process consists of the key performance indicators you use, the group and individual performance targets set, and the way performance is reviewed, encouraged and rewarded against these targets. The informal performance management approach is tied up on a day-to-day basis with the way staff are managed and motivated.

Performance management starts informally with simple things: how you praise and thank staff, and what you applaud them for – or conversely criticise them for and what you encourage them to stop.

How well the informal performance management process works is dependent on the behaviour of managers, especially the very senior ones.

Management behaviour needs to be seen to be consistent with the change. Inconsistent behaviour is exhibited through the mentality of 'do what I say, not do what I do'. Whatever your senior executives do will become the established behaviour of the organisation, and so it needs to be consistent with whatever you are trying to achieve. For example, there's little point trying to make your staff cost conscious if your senior executives blatantly are not. Conversely, if your senior managers are always polite and on time for meetings, staff will tend to be polite and on time for meetings.

At times it can be difficult to be continuously consistent with a change. For example, you could be changing culture and as part of this change you are encouraging openness and honesty. Honesty and openness are great things to value, but it does not take too much imagination to consider situations in which this is difficult or even impossible to achieve. If your change programme is changing or emphasising principles of work and organisational values you must toil hard to be seen explicitly to be acting consistently to the spirit of those principles and values. However, staff are intelligent and understand that no guiding principles are absolute and that occasionally you have to work in a way that is contrary to change. It will be noticed when you do – so whenever you work in a contrary fashion explain and make it clear that it is an exception for exceptional reasons.

Performance is also driven by your formal performance management mechanisms including appraisal, rewards and bonus systems, and it is backed up by the way you choose who to promote. Modern organisations realise that money, rewards and promotions are not the only way to motivate people, but they are certainly important contributory factors.

Unless both informal and formal performance management is aligned with the change you have made, then you risk it slowly (or quickly!) becoming undone. Every time you praise a member of staff for work that is counter to the change, you undermine the change. Every time a manager, especially a senior executive, behaves in a way that is opposed to the change, it will start to roll back your hard work. Every time someone is rewarded for work that is in conflict with the change, you enforce the point that the change is to be ignored. Whenever you promote a member of staff who works contrary to the change, you really confirm the irrelevance of the change. However, each time a member of staff is rewarded for behaving in a way that is consistent with the change, it reinforces it and makes it stronger.

Staff do not always like change, but understand that an organisation must change to thrive. They will find it hard to adopt the change unless you manage performance in line with the change. After all, your performance management system is there explicitly to encourage certain behaviour, and if the behaviour you want to encourage has changed so must your performance management approach. Ideally the design and implementation of a revised performance management approach is not considered as an afterthought, but developed as a core component of your change project.

Step 7.2 Help people adapt

People's ability to adapt to change is varied. It will take different lengths of time for people really to settle into a change and, depending on the nature of the change, to understand how much someone's role has been modified and the degree of alteration in behaviour required.

The key point is therefore that support, especially from direct line managers, for individuals to adapt to change cannot end on the day when a change is deemed to have been implemented. Support for individuals should end when people's need for support ends. This can often be long after the formal change project is considered as complete. Helping staff adapt to change is a key role of managers. Making the team alert to upcoming change, monitoring the team's reaction to change, assisting the team to understand fully the rationale for change, and supporting the education and training of individual staff are all parts of a line manager's normal responsibility.

In the end some people will never adapt to some changes, and if the change is in the best interest of your organisation then it is time for your organisation and these people to part company. Parting company in a professional and mutually acceptable way can be difficult, but it is worth the effort to make it as easy as possible for people to leave. Anyone who is forced out of an organisation risks being a strong detractor, and possibly an active force against the organisation. People who are treated with dignity and realistic termination payments are more likely to maintain a positive image of an organisation.

As an extreme example of a company going out of its way to help someone adapt to change, I met a man who six months after being asked to leave a business was sent a letter thanking him for his time with the organisation, and enclosing a cheque with his annual bonus. This is an extreme case, and many organisations could not afford to do this, but the result was that someone who was made redundant remained a strong and active advocate of the organisation.

Step 7.3 Admit mistakes

Even the best intentioned change can turn out to be a mistake. This may be realised immediately, but for some changes it is only several months after implementation that it is realised that the change or some component of the change was a mistake. When a mistake has been made it is best to admit it and make a subsequent modification. To admit a mistake requires two things.

Firstly, you must know you have made a mistake, and this requires the measurement of performance following a change. The need for the data and performance metrics you collected during your change does not stop once the change is complete, but is an ongoing requirement. Another way to identify mistakes is by analysing what people do on a day-to-day basis. If this is the same as before the change, the change has not worked. This may seem obvious, but it is surprisingly common for people to be doing exactly the same work in the same way after a change project is supposedly complete.

Secondly, it requires confidence and humility to admit the mistake and make subsequent changes. Management and leadership culture can often make admitting mistakes difficult, as making a mistake is considered equivalent to failure. Successful organisations, especially commercial enterprises, have to be willing to take risks to thrive. Taking risk means that sometimes you will make a mistake. Obviously you cannot make too many mistakes, but making none at all is more likely to be as a consequence of avoiding risk altogether rather than brilliant foresight and planning.

Making occasional mistakes is not failure, but failure to admit mistakes is! Hidden mistakes risks damaging your organisation as you rectify the situation. It also develops a culture of cynicism in your staff. When a major mistake has been made your staff will know. Better to own up and move on, than to wallow in it pretending nothing is wrong. No one wants to work for someone who continually makes mistakes, but people value managers who in between their successes are willing to put up their hands and admit when they got it wrong.

Mistakes need to be revised and reworked and another change implemented to overcome them. The need to change is never finished; there will be another change programme and so the opportunity to fix mistakes is always there.

Step 7.4 End the change

Change in a general sense never ends, but any one specific change has to come to an end, and the end should be planned. The reason you need to understand when a change is complete is so you can determine when you can release resources working on the change. Additionally, you need to know when your organisation's management and leadership team can stop you spending time working on this change.

The end point is never absolutely clear, and requires some degree of judgement. It is not simply about reaching the end of a project's defined timeline, as change is about achieving results, not completing a set of tasks on a plan. Change normally needs time to consolidate after implementation, time to bed in and become the normal way of working. The ultimate test of completion is when what was initially perceived as a change has become the standard unquestioned way for your organisation to operate, what is often referred to as 'business as usual'. Unfortunately, this is generally not a clear-cut point, and given the pace of change in most organisations you cannot meaningfully wait for this time.

Releasing the change team will start when the change goes live, but the whole team may not be released for some time. It is normally best to stagger the release of team members, and this needs to be planned in advance as they may assume that they are free from the point of going live. The reason you will need to keep some of them subsequently is to support staff who are finding the change difficult, to overcome any final problems that arise at the point of implementation, and to perform any action to help consolidate the change in the organisation. In terms of timing, many staff will be able to be released as soon as implementation has occurred, but for major changes some support may be required for several months after implementation.

Planning and preparation for the phase after going live is essential, and if you want your change to be a success you may require robust support from the change manager and the change sponsor. There is always pressure in organisations to release resources from projects, either for staff to go back to their normal jobs, or to move on to the next project. Unless it is explained well, senior managers will assume that as soon as a change has occurred any resources they have provided to the project will come back to them. However, the 'bedding-in' phase after going live is important. Occasionally a major problem will arise, but many of the issues found after going live will be individually trivial. If not fixed, many issues can, cumulatively, have a major negative effect on performance. This is especially true when there are a continuous series of changes and bugs, snags, issues and irritations are never resolved.

From a management perspective a change is complete when the objectives you set out to achieve have been achieved, or your organisation has accepted that these objectives will not be achieved and has made an explicit decision to move on. Objectives in organisations evolve, and once an objective has been reached it is yesterday's solution to yesterday's problem. Management have a limited capacity and cannot focus on every measure and every facet of an organisation. Once an objective is achieved, attention can be reduced and focused on today's problem and the search for today's solution. The balance to find is to ensure that yesterday's work is properly complete before moving on to today's and tomorrow's workload. If this is not done change will unravel.

Key tips

- Ensure that the way you manage and motivate staff is consistent with your change. Performance management needs to be modified and aligned to change.

- Accept that people take time to adapt to change, and different people will adapt at different speeds.
- Admit and rectify mistakes as soon as you are aware of them. Do not deny or ignore them, hoping they will go away or be unobserved.
- Plan for the end of your change and the most appropriate scheduled release of resources working on the change.

TO DO NOW

- Identify what in your organisation's performance management approach is consistent with the change you are implementing, and what is in conflict.

- Determine what components of your performance management approach need to be modified to match your change.

- Ensure your change plan takes account of post-implementation activities and the resources required to undertake them.

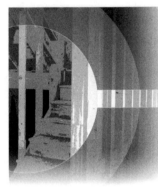

Step 8

Manage communications

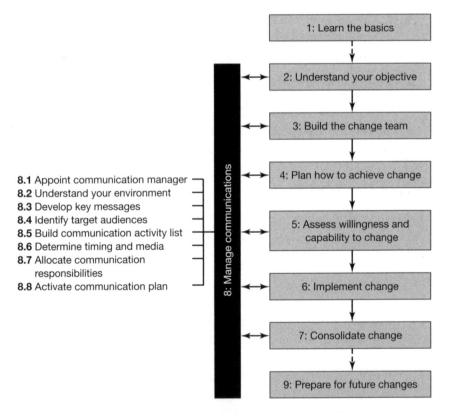

	1: Learn the basics
	2: Understand your objective
	3: Build the change team
8.1 Appoint communication manager	4: Plan how to achieve change
8.2 Understand your environment	
8.3 Develop key messages	
8.4 Identify target audiences	5: Assess willingness and capability to change
8.5 Build communication activity list	
8.6 Determine timing and media	
8.7 Allocate communication responsibilities	6: Implement change
8.8 Activate communication plan	7: Consolidate change
	9: Prepare for future changes

8: Manage communications

THIS CHAPTER COVERS:

- Delivering pertinent and timely communication to support your change.

THE CENTRAL POINT IS:

- Communication is essential to change management, and in some situations change management is communication management. Communication is crucial in developing readiness and enthusiasm for change, in modifying the way people think and behave, in education and training, and in ensuring change continues to be adhered to after implementation. Communication for change is a two-way process and is as much about listening and gathering information as transmitting key messages. Good change communication starts by using the informal and unstructured communication that goes on all the time. Staff and managers are educated to make what they say consistent with the overall message of change. But change communication also uses formal planned communication events and listening sessions. Good change communication significantly improves the likelihood of success and can considerably reduce the risk from change.

Setting the scene

Consider the following three examples of communication about a change, which show the impact of inadequate or inconsistent information sharing upon change.

1. The COO of a business decided to improve the processes used by its customer services division. Customer services was made up of a number of departments including: customer order taking, answering customer queries and resolving customer complaints. Most of the work was done through a series of call centres taking thousands of customer calls every day. The staff in the call centres were meant to work according to a documented set of processes and procedures, but these were felt to be out of date and unsuited to the expectations of modern consumers. The existing processes were a mixture of documented procedures which were inflexible and often did not allow staff to meet customer needs, whilst in other areas there were no processes at all, which led to highly inconsistent customer service. A change programme was started to redesign all the processes and procedures to enable all customers to be served flexibly whilst maintaining consistency of approach. A team was pulled together to design and document the improved processes. It was given a suite of rooms in a separate building from customer services so it could focus on its work without interruption. The team worked for several months to design the processes, and was very pleased with the results. At the end of six months they were ready for implementation. The processes started to be rolled out to the staff to use. Very quickly a huge number of comments came back to the design team, typified by statements like: 'These will never work', 'Why have these been designed?', 'Who asked us?' 'Why wasn't anyone involved?' Several weeks after implementation staff were still using their old procedures, commenting 'We don't really know what the new ones are for, so we have ignored them'.

2. The IT manager in an organisation was going to implement a new system which would impact on many of the people in the organisation. To ensure everyone was aware of the work she gave a formal presentation every fortnight in the staff canteen on Friday between 10 and 11 am. The presentations gave very clear status updates, set expectations as to the impact of the change, and reminded everyone of the project's objectives. Some of her colleagues thought these sessions were excellent, and told her that they had never been so well informed about an upcoming change. Others, though, were less complimentary. Typical comments were: 'What about the staff who are not based in this building?', 'What about people who are not free from 10 to 11 am on Fridays?', 'PowerPoint is not the best way to explain the project to all of our staff'.

3. A well-regarded operational manager was asked to run a change programme. Although he had not run such a programme before, as an operational manager he had been affected by many, or in his terms, 'suffered from fools who don't know how to implement anything'. He understood the need to communicate well, and decided to ensure there were regular conversations with all staff about every aspect of the change programme. To ensure dialogue happened as regularly and as quickly as he felt was needed, he encouraged everyone in the change team to talk all the time to all staff about the change. After this change programme was over no one was going to

be able to accuse him of insufficient communications. The programme progressed and there were continual interactions between members of the change team and the rest of the organisation. To ensure all the communication was happening that was required, the manager decided to go and ask staff from a range of functions if they knew everything they felt they needed to. He was surprised to receive comments like, 'We are told lots, but it does not really make sense', 'We were told yesterday by one person that the programme would be over in June, but someone else told us today that it is not until October', 'Are we really making that many people redundant?', 'I've spent a lot of time listening to presentations which frankly were irrelevant to me', 'I don't want to know anything more about this programme unless it really is useful!'

It is obvious that the change programmes in all these examples would be helped by better communication. In the first example the problem is that there really was no communication. The staff were not consulted about or involved in the change. As a result they were not expecting and not prepared for the change, and did not have the opportunity to comment on the work. Without any dialogue staff expectations cannot be managed, people are not prepared for the change, and the change team does not get the opportunity to obtain the comments of experienced staff on its work. A lot of great work can be wasted because of a lack of communication.

In the second example there was some communication, but it was inadequate for all the affected staff's needs. Although what and how the IT director presented was good in its own right, it was insufficient for all staff. In any organisation there are a wide range of people with quite different communication needs. For communication to be successful it has to be relevant to the audience and be done in a way that is understandable and acceptable to that audience. Communication must be tailored in terms of style, format, media and timing to suit different audiences.

In the final example there was a huge amount of information provided, perhaps too much. The problem with uncontrolled discussions is that you can never be sure what message is being communicated. In the second example you saw the need for communication to be tailored to the audience. But however many audiences you have, the basic messages have to be consistent. Good change communication is done in a controlled way to ensure that everyone knows what they need to know, when they need to know it, but also with confidence that what they are being told is correct. On a large change team there will be different views of what is important, and what the current status of the change project is. If communication is not controlled you can end up confusing your audience. Additionally, without adequate control and co-ordination staff may have inappropriate information passed to them. The way to achieve this control of communication starts by having allocated responsibility for communications management.

There are two statements that can be heard in one form or another across most change projects. The staff affected by the change will say that 'there was not enough communication, no one told us anything', and the change team will say 'we communicated all the time, but we can only communicate what we are ready to communicate'. Great communication aims to balance these two views, getting to a point where everyone is satisfied that they know what they need to know when they want to know it.

Introduction to communication

One of the most important factors differentiating between well and badly implemented change is the quality, quantity and appropriateness of your communications. Although there is a balance between saying too much and too little, the principle you should work to is that you cannot tell staff enough and you must communicate ceaselessly. But good communication is not simply about good intentions to talk regularly; it is about deliberate, timely and structured messages to achieve a known end result.

Why is communication so important? Communication enables:

- *The management of people's expectations*: good communication raises awareness and support for change, and even the most unpopular changes will occur more smoothly when people are prepared for them. With unpopular changes prompt information enables you to manage responses. There are good and bad times to explain change, and part of communications planning is to determine when these times are, but very rare is the project when it is best not to communicate and so manage expectations.

- *Staff to determine if they are doing the right things*: unless staff understand why a change is happening they cannot be sure if their own actions and behaviours are consistent with the change.

- *Certain change to occur*: communication can propel change by starting a positive response. Once a message is understood and accepted, people's behaviour will start to modify. If you continuously say what is important in an organisation, and then support this with positive feedback, behaviour will tend to move towards what you desire. Cultural change programmes are predominantly about modifying performance management combined with appropriate and continuous communication.

- *The collection of feedback on change*: your staff will provide an excellent source of information, suggestions and constructive ideas about change. Without listening you will not collect this essential feedback.

- *Comprehension, attitudes and responses to the change to be understood*: managing change requires managing responses. If you do not listen, you will not understand the response you should be managing. You will also not understand how good your staff's comprehension of the change is.

- *Some deliverables to be implemented*: the core mechanism for training and education is communication.

Communication will not happen by itself and is not resource free. It is a major activity on most change initiatives. For the bigger changes you may need dedicated resources with specialist communication skills. If you are lucky enough to work in an organisation with an internal communications department you will be calling on its resources. It is critical to perform your communication well and use the skills available. When communication is well designed and executed it will be a major help; poorly designed and executed communication can be a disaster.

There can be a tendency to try to use communication to gloss over the unpleasant truth of change. Change should be done for the interests of an organisation. Unfortunately the wider and long-term interests of organisations rarely align with those of all stakeholders, including staff. Good communication can help prepare people for change, and can moderate any negative responses. A role of communication is to sell the benefits of change to staff, but communication should not be used to try and convince staff that a change is in their interest if it is not. Put more bluntly, you should not let your attempts to sell change veer into lying. Although lying can remove short-term problems it is best avoided. Staff are likely to be even more negative when they feel they have been misled, and may cease believing what they are told by managers and leaders. Always identify negatively impacted groups, and honestly advise them as much in advance as is practical of the change.

Some of the factors to consider in communication are the message to be transmitted, the media that will be used, the target audience for this message and the timing. In change situations it is also vital to ensure that communication flows both ways. Good communication planning sets up the mechanisms to encourage and allow information to be received in a usable format.

Encouraging an effective two-way dialogue often means more frequent smaller conversations, rather than once-off large presentations. As part of this you must continually check for comprehension. Just because you have passed information does not mean you have been heard or understood. Information must be repeated until you are sure the messages are fully understood. This is easier the earlier in your change project you start discussing it with affected staff. Also you must check what staff want to know, and do not assume this is simply the same as what you require them to know. Tell them why you are changing, what you are changing and how you are changing, and then ask them what further they want to know.

Communication happens both informally and formally. We all talk and listen to people on an ongoing basis. Just because the conversation in these situations is informal does not mean it cannot be useful and adapted to the goals of change. You will benefit greatly by using ongoing informal and unstructured discussions. Obviously, you cannot pre-plan all the chat that happens in your offices. So, to make use of informal communications the important messages of your change need to be within your managers' minds, so that when they talk they naturally reflect the change and use the language of the change. Additionally, informal dialogue is where most feedback arises. Managers need to be alert for useful comments and reactions to the change and have a mechanism to pass this on to the change team. Secondly, change management programmes usually need formal communication events in the activity plan. Such events may consist of anything from major presentations by the chief executive to the whole organisation through to an email to a specific group of people with some information about the change.

Don't worry if you are not a great orator or writer – good communication is not about having a way with words, although this will help, it is about understanding what you are trying to achieve, having a comprehensive supporting communication plan, and about following this throughout your change process. It is about predicting needs and planning for them, but it is also about quick responses to altering situations. The communication activities must be designed to support your specific change.

The activities in this step run parallel to the rest of the steps in this book. Communication starts when you are forming objectives, and continues after implementation until the change is fully consolidated. Communication will support or even drive the events in your change plan, and will need to take place throughout the life of your project. Communication has been separated out from the other steps to emphasise its importance. Steps 8.1 to 8.8 are shown as a linear process, and the order of steps shown here is logical. However, in practice you are likely to iterate between the steps as the change initiative progresses.

The step-by-step guide
Step 8 – Manage communications

Step 8.1 Appoint communication manager

Communication is often wrapped up in the mystique of an exclusive skill that only certain people have. There are special communication skills, and you may need to call on them, but in the context of a change, project communication starts as a list of tasks that need to be done. Like any other activity, it needs people to do the tasks and someone to manage them. The *doing* part of communication will be shared across many people in the organisation, especially the change team and line managers, but it must be *managed*. Often the communication's management responsibility falls to the change manager, and it can be seen as one part of his or her overall role. However, for a large and complex change, or a change that requires a significant amount of communication, it may be necessary to have a dedicated communication manager working for the change manager.

The communication manager is not required specifically to define and implement every conversation, presentation or feedback session. He or she must ensure that there is a comprehensive communication plan, that this plan and the communication it delivers is consistent with the change being implemented, that there are sufficient resources to perform the communication required, and that the execution and completion of all the tasks in the communications plan are managed. An internal communications or PR skill set is not essential, but is advantageous.

The communication manager is therefore part project manager, part change manager and part communication specialist. If this sounds like it is a big challenge, it can be! However, it is not something anyone should panic about. With a sensible plan, a good understanding of the change and by applying common sense, communication management is not a daunting task.

Sharing information and gathering feedback are important to all changes, but the role of the communication manager becomes most critical on changes which involve prolonged communications across an organisation, such as cultural change programmes.

Step 8.2 Understand your environment

Before developing a communication plan it is helpful, and sometimes essential, to have a good understanding of the environment and culture of your organisation, and any rules or constraints concerning how and when information should be shared. Where external consultants are used to support communication, it is important that they develop presentations and documentation which are relevant and appropriate to your organisation. To achieve this they have to work closely with your own staff. It is up to the communication manager to ensure that there is adequate understanding of your organisation's environment.

The factors that need to be considered in a communication plan can be many and varied. Start by determining if there are any legal or regulatory constraints, rules or guidelines about what, how and when communications can be made. Legal and regulatory guidance often can have an impact on the timing of communications, and require specific individuals or groups to be warned beforehand and consulted prior to a change. Such constraints and rules may relate to:

- *Financial transactions*: which in most jurisdictions are tightly governed by a range of regulations. If you are about to undergo a merger, or announce results that can affect share price, the rules governing how and when you communicate this can be quite onerous.

- *HR*: there are many rules relating to communicating change to staff. For example, there are rules governing notice periods for redundancy or outsourcing of staff.

- *Health and safety*: such regulations can be relevant in some instances. For example, requirements to educate a workforce to use new machinery in a safe way.

- *Contract law*: which is relevant if your change has an impact on supplier or customer contracts. These often have minimum times of prior warning and for agreeing modifications.

- *Specific regulations regarding your industry*: some industries, including utilities and the financial sector, have rules about who must be informed and consulted on certain changes, and how long in advance of a change this must occur.

Beyond the conditions of the law there may be a looser set of guiding principles, agreements and cultural norms which, although not absolute rules, should be adhered to. Again, such guiding principles often can affect the timing of communication, and require specific individuals or groups to be warned beforehand and consulted prior to a change. Considerations of that type include the following:

- Do you have any agreements with staff forums or unions to alert them in advance to change, or to consult about change? Are these relevant to the change you are making?

- Is this change going to affect directly or be visible to your customers? Do you want to or have to alert or consult your customers?

- Is this change going to affect directly or be visible to any of your suppliers? Will the change have an impact on any contracts which you must discuss with your suppliers? Is there a chance your suppliers will be unsettled or worried about the change, and if so do you want to alert or consult with them first to try and mitigate this?

- Are there any other stakeholder groups you have to or should discuss the change with?

Additionally, your organisation has its own processes and culture which can affect or shape the style, timing and approach to communications. In relation to these you may ask the following questions:

- What are the procedural rules or cultural norms for communication in your organisation? Do you tend to communicate early, or is it normal to communicate only when a message is fully formed? What media do you use: email, voicemail, letters or face-to-face sessions? What do you say to groups and what on a one-to-one basis?

- What communications channels exist in your organisation? Are there existing newsletters, team briefing sessions, regular meetings that can or should be used to share change information?

- Does the change you are making influence the way you must communicate? For example, a change to drive greater openness in an organisation will not be taken seriously unless it is supported by open communication.

By asking questions of the type identified in this section the communication manager can start to develop a list of factors that have to be included within the communication plan. For instance:

- *Specific communication to identified groups*: this includes other stakeholders, such as shareholders, consumers, government bodies, who need to have change communicated to them.

- *Timing constraints and dependencies*: these may be between tasks in the communication plan, but equally may be on other events in the overall change plan. Sometimes seemingly trivial details can, because of legal or regulatory reasons, drive the timing of events in a change plan and consequently the timing of communications. For example, if your customers pay their bills by direct debit (DD) and you wish to make a modification to such payments, you have to alert customers with a minimum notice period defined by the banks. This means that if you are changing anything in your processes, product line-up or pricing that concerns customers' DDs, you must communicate in advance.

- *Media and format guidance*: for example, certain information has to be provided in a written format, other facts you may only want to pass on verbally.

Step 8.3 Develop key messages

The central building block of your communication plan is a series of messages that you need to transmit and collect responses to, driven by your core change plan. Before creating any message you should ask yourself why you are undertaking any specific activity and what you will achieve by communicating about it – so what do you need to say? Unless you are clear about this, your communication risks being inconsistent and possibly incoherent.

If you are performing some form of cultural or behavioural change, the key messages will have been developed as an integral part of that work. For many other changes it is also necessary to think through what the key messages are. By key messages I mean the fundamental ideas underpinning a change that you want to build up and repeat throughout the change programme until they are universally accepted. The sorts of key messages to develop include answers to the following questions:

- What is going to be changed and what will be different once the change is complete?
- What is the rationale for this change? Why is the change the right thing to do?
- Why is this specific solution a great way to meet this rationale?
- Why does this change have to be done now? Why is this the right or best time for the change?

Additionally, you may regard it as crucially important to have common and consistent messages which effectively answer the following questions:

- How will this change affect the people in the organisation? There is not usually a fixed answer to this question: the answer will evolve as your change progresses and as it becomes appropriate to share information with staff. However, this does not mean you cannot inform staff. You should say what you know when you know it, and say what questions you cannot yet answer.

- How will the people in the organisation be supported through the change? This may seem a peripheral question, but it is important. Staff will often be as worried about how they will be treated as what actually is going to happen to them. They are much more likely to be supportive and calm about change when they know, and have it consistently reinforced, that they will be treated fairly and professionally, and the organisation will help anyone negatively affected to the best of its ability. This is not about stating that no one is worse off from change, but clearly stating that there will be appropriate levels of support.

- How important is the change? Is the change a core activity that takes precedence over anything else that is being worked on, or is it a lower priority activity that needs to be fitted around current work when there is time? Again this may seem like a peripheral question, but if a change is really important and needs to be completed quickly then everyone needs to know that work on it is a priority. Alternatively, if you do not want anyone stopping current work to support your change you should make this clear.

Step 8.4 Identify target audiences

Next you must consider which parts of your organisation will be affected by the change, and break this up into sensible groupings for targeted messages. (The identification of target audiences is complementary to step 5.) The balance you need to strike is that from a workload perspective you want to communicate in a common way to as a wide an audience as possible, yet on the other hand communication is most effective when it is tailored to the individual being spoken to.

A good way to determine your target audience starts with an organisation chart. Ignore any parts of the organisation that are not affected by the change, that are unlikely to try to have an impact on or influence the change, and that do not need to know about the change for any other reason. What you are left with is your total target audience. The most efficient way to communicate is to develop common presentations and documentation which can be disseminated to the whole of this group. However, efficient is not necessarily effective. You may have to tailor communications to different audiences. To decide whether you should break the audience into smaller groups ask yourself:

- Does the content of the message need to vary between groups? Different teams may need different information. Staff who benefit from change will definitely need a different approach from those for whom it is detrimental. It is insensitive to celebrate change and create enthusiasm for an audience that includes people who will lose their jobs as a result of the change. Unfortunately, I have seen it done many times.

- Does the level of detail required vary from group to group? Managers may need more information than their staff, as will those who need to change their work compared with those who simply need to be aware that a change has been made.

- What is the most appropriate type of language, format and media for a message to a specific group? Communicating to a group of dispersed field-based sales staff may need to be done in a different way from a team of accountants based in a central office.

You need to apply common sense and judgement in deciding upon your target audiences. If you are making a minor change then communication needs to be simple and cost effective, and you may even envisage something as easy and cheap as a single email to the whole organisation. On the other hand, if the change is complex and affects many different groups in different ways, you may need to divide your target audience into lots of sub-groups (tens of different groups are not unusual), each of which will receive tailored communication, possibly in different formats from different sources.

In identifying your target audiences remember that you are not only seeking to identify which audiences you need to speak to, but also those you should be listening to. The purpose of such listening is to gain feedback on the content of the change, on the progress of delivering and implementing change, and on the impact the change is having once implemented.

When you do ask for feedback, make sure that you use it. Feedback will provide powerful information. Gathering feedback to make staff feel they are being consulted and then ignoring it usually backfires. That is not to say you have to use every piece of it. On receiving feedback thank staff for it, even if it is negative and difficult to respond to. Where it will not be used tell staff this, and tell them why you will not use it. Where feedback is criticism try and determine what is being criticised precisely – is it the underlying objective of the change, the solution to meet this objective or how the change project is being run? Unless criticism is understood, it is almost impossible to respond constructively to it.

There are multiple channels for feedback, including face-to-face conversations, conference calls, group sessions and email. For feedback to be most useful to a change team it needs both to be structured, as this aids analysis, and to allow freeform comments.

Step 8.5 Build communication activity list

The next stage is to convert what you want to communicate and to whom into a list of defined activities. These activities are to transmit all of the key messages identified in step 8.3 to each of the target audiences identified in step 8.4 at the most appropriate time. You will use this list of activities to build your communication plan. Essentially you want to create a comprehensive set of all the different communication activities that need to be done to support adequately your change initiative.

The list of activities you develop should comprehensively and repeatedly provide information to and gather information from each target audience group until you are confident that the key messages you want to transmit have been fully and completely understood. Additionally, take the following points into consideration when developing your activity list:

- Will you be implementing any quick wins (see step 4), which you need to leverage to gain a positive response?
- What information and tools (e.g. presentations, frequently asked questions or FAQs, etc.) do you need to develop and give your line management to enable them to support their staff through the life of the change?

- What do people need to be warned of beforehand?
- When and who should you be consulting? How are you going to perform this consultation?
- What do people need encouragement in to keep involved?
- When should you be listening for responses? How will you collect these responses?
- Once the change is implemented, what communication needs to be made to ensure it does not unravel?
- What feedback should you collect after implementation?
- Will there be any requirement for longer term feedback on the change?
- What specific communication events, and constraints or dependencies on other activities, arose from the work in step 8.2?
- What messages are you happy for your change team and line management to transmit informally – and what information must not be communicated in this way?

Step 8.6 Determine timing and media

You now know what you want to communicate, who you want to communicate to, and what the key communication activities are. To convert these into a communication plan you must finally identify when you will communicate and the media you will use.

The multiple media you have available will have different levels of suitability. For example, email is great for mass communications, but not for sensitive interactions. Voicemail messages may be appropriate for office-based staff, but may be less useful for home-workers. To alert staff to events, text messages and instant messengers can be used, but they cannot provide detailed information and should not be used for sensitive information. Sensitive information is really best dealt with on a one-to-one basis. Often there will be communication standards in the organisation, especially if change is a common occurrence.

Timing of communication is critical. Identifying the most appropriate time is about balancing between communicating too early in a change project, when you may not have enough detail to explain everything staff will want to know, and communicating too late, when staff will complain you have kept them in the dark.

If staff find out about a major change before you communicate it you have no opportunity to set the tone and try to manage the response. The challenge is to communicate openly, honestly and as early as possible, whilst being aware of the possible impact of communication, and the impact of communicating when you do not have a fully formed message to communicate. It is a difficult balance to find, and one you will almost certainly get wrong at times. You will get no thanks for warning people about a change you cannot explain in detail because you have not done all the work in steps 4 and 5. But at the same time you will receive criticism for not warning people about change if you wait until you know about it in detail. In planning communication you have to decide on the best balance between these two extremes. One point to bear in mind is that you can always tell staff you do not yet have the answer to all questions, by being open in indicating that change will happen, but being clear that not all of the details have been defined.

A critical factor in controlling information is what and when you allow to be communicated informally compared with what must only be communicated formally. Although informal communications, essentially letting the change team talk to whoever it interacts with, are powerful and useful, they must not be used for certain information. For example, the initial announcement of the dates and timings of redundancy must be done formally. To make best use of informal communications you must make absolutely clear what *cannot* be transmitted in this way.

Another factor in deciding the timing of communication is the impact of other events outside an individual change project. You may be able to leverage other events to help you communicate. If your organisation already has planned presentations bringing together large parts of your target audience, why not also use these events to communicate about your specific change? On the other hand, other events may restrict when you want to communicate. If your change is only one of several, you have to consider the total message staff will be getting from all changes. There is no point trying to get staff upbeat and excited about your change when another change project is announcing bad news.

Step 8.7 Allocate communication responsibilities

The final component of your communication plan is to identify who will be responsible for creating and for delivering each of the communication activities you have identified. You are looking for appropriate people with adequate communication skills.

To select the right people for each communication you can consider the following points:

- Who is available and has the correct skills and knowledge to create any communication materials?
- Who is actually available and willing to deliver the communication?
- What communication will be done by the change team and what needs to be done by line managers as part of their normal role? Line managers are often the most appropriate people to communicate changes to their teams, and it is often impractical for a change team to try and communicate directly to the whole organisation. This normally means that line managers have to be briefed before their staff. Communication planning often includes cascades of information from one layer in the management hierarchy to another and then throughout the organisation. This can be logistically demanding and require close control and timing.
- Who is the most credible source of information? Some communications need to come from the chief executive or another senior executive. For other communications the most credible source may be staff representatives.

Step 8.8 Activate communication plan

When your communication plan is completed it should be run like any other set of activities in your change project. The activities need to be done in a timely fashion and co-ordinated with the schedule in the change plan. Progress relative to the communication plan should be measured, and if anything is delayed you need to catch up. Dependencies between communication events and other change activities need to be monitored and co-ordination maintained. The effect of communication needs to be assessed, and if it does not achieve its goal further communication needs to be undertaken. Flexibility and responsiveness need to be maintained as things will happen during your change that you have not planned for and which will need some form of communication response.

As you work through your communication plan you must remain alert to what is happening. Things you have not predicted will happen. Some information will be received exactly as you expected, and some will not work as well as planned. A communication plan is not a recipe that is followed exactly, but needs to be adapted and amended as reality occurs.

Take care with communicating your critical messages. You may have only one chance to get vital communication right. If you mess it up you may cause major problems. This does not mean you can shy away or delay communication events, it means you must put the effort into getting them correct.

Deciding and planning communication is one thing, executing it successfully is quite another! The language of communication should be both appropriate and meaningful to your audience. Terminology should be understood or explained to every audience. If the message is upbeat use upbeat language; if it is downbeat, avoid upbeat language!

As part of changing people's behaviour, attitudes or styles of working it is often necessary to introduce new concepts, and this may require using new terminology. But do not fall into the trap of mistaking jargon for interesting or useful information. Staff will be irritated or amused, but not motivated, by the simple application of jargon. This can be a specific problem when external consultants are used to support change. Ask them to use your language not their jargon if it is not appropriate to your organisation.

Communication tends to be associated with what we say and hear, and what we write and read. Never forget that communication is much more than this, and every action taken communicates. The phrase 'actions speak louder than words' may be old and unoriginal, but it is true. Presenting on the need to cut costs when an executive is seen to be spending lavishly, or explaining the desire to have a culture of respect when a senior manager is repeatedly rude, will completely remove any benefit from the communication. Communication will be partially or completely undermined unless the behaviour of managers and leaders in the organisation is consistent with what is communicated.

Additionally, communication is more than words. We all transmit and receive information all the time from the way we interact and from various non-verbal behaviours such as tone of voice, facial expressions and body posture. Great communications requires consistency between what is said and the associated body language.

Key tips

- In most change projects communication is one of the most important activities and should be treated as such.

- Communication should be deliberate, co-ordinated and consistent with the overall change across the lifetime of the change.

- Communication materials need to be as broad as possible to minimise workload, but as specific as possible and tailored to individual audiences to have an impact. Deciding between these two extremes is an important decision for the communication manager.

- Communication can spur the uptake of change, but communicating about change should not be mistaken for taking action.

TO DO NOW

- If you are new to the organisation ensure you understand any rules, guidelines or norms for communicating.

- Make sure you are aware of any other changes happening in parallel that may have an impact on your communication plan.

- Identify what resources your organisation has available to support your change communication.

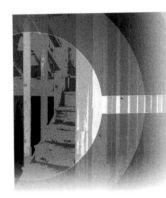

Step 9

Prepare for future changes

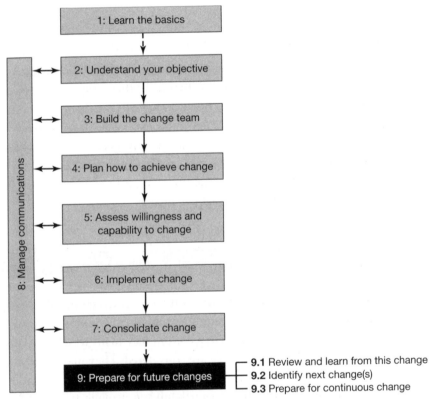

1: Learn the basics

2: Understand your objective

3: Build the change team

4: Plan how to achieve change

5: Assess willingness and capability to change

6: Implement change

7: Consolidate change

8: Manage communications

9: Prepare for future changes
- **9.1** Review and learn from this change
- **9.2** Identify next change(s)
- **9.3** Prepare for continuous change

THIS CHAPTER COVERS:

- Developing the skills and capabilities for continuous change.

THE CENTRAL POINT IS:

- The capability to change quickly and effectively is essential for the long-term survival of any organisation. This capability can be developed by learning from the experience of change, having an ongoing expectation and readiness for change, ensuring there are the necessary change management skills available, and developing flexibility in all components of the organisation to ensure change can be achieved rapidly.

Setting the scene

It is astonishing how often I am involved with organisations which struggle with change. This would not be surprising if these organisations were facing change for the first time, but the majority of them have made changes almost continuously. Well-managed organisations tend to become good at the things they do frequently because management attention is focused on those activities, and because the skills and experience of the staff increase. However, this does not seem to apply in the same way to change and change management.

No doubt organisations which go through change are often better at managing it than those which go through change rarely. However, it is unusual to come across organisations that really excel at change. I have come across organisations in which staff are used to change, in which managers see change as part of their jobs, and in which the leadership team promotes the cause of change – but the organisations still do not excel. This is most telling when large consultancy firms which specialise in helping firms adapt and change are considered. They may be great at advising others, but in my experience, when their own organisations change, for example through mergers, they often struggle as hard as their clients to make the transition to their desired state.

In my opinion, one of the key reasons for this difficulty is the treatment of change as a single transaction, whereas increasingly change needs to be looked upon holistically as an ongoing series of modifications to an organisation. Another major point is that change management skills are not always developed in a conscious and deliberate manner as other management skills. This chapter provides some guidance on how to start achieving excellence in change management.

Introduction to preparing for future changes

If you have completed the activities in steps 1 to 8 your change should be complete. This step takes you further and helps you to develop the skills for ongoing change.

There has been much written in the management literature concerning the increasing pace of change. I accept this, though in truth I have seen little objective and measurable evidence of this phenomenon. It just feels intuitively correct. What is undoubtedly true is that there is a constant requirement to change driven by a range of factors such as increased competition, technology development, globalisation, rising customer expectations and environmental concerns.

Most activity in organisations is normally managed through one of two main mechanisms – business processes, whether formally called such, and project management. Business processes manage the normal day-to-day repeated activities of the organisations, and managers are increasingly adept at driving and improving performance in processes. Project management is used to deliver the once-off activities which do not fit into the framework of a process. Changes may be formally run as projects using the full range of project management tools, or they may more informally use what I call a project mindset. A project mindset is the approach to delivering activities as unique series of events going through the steps of thinking, planning, doing and finishing.

The approach to change described in this book looks upon change from the perspective of an individual change, and considers the individual change in the framework of a project. If you have worked through the steps up to the end of step 8 you have done enough to deliver the change. However, as change becomes continuous it is helpful to look at change as something that must be delivered more like a business process. Each change remains unique and a project mindset is core to delivery, but there are many repeated steps and activities in most changes that can be developed into a repeatable process.

An example of processes being put in place to deliver continuous change is the way some organisations have defined new product development (NPD) as a repeatable process. This is a way of combining both the benefits of a repeatable process and a common series of steps. In some cases permanently allocated staff are used to deliver those steps. Project management is used to give robust management of progress and risk through the process which in every instance will be working to different requirements, take different lengths of time, and use different amounts of resources.

A feature of processes is the ability to embed continuous performance improvement. Every iteration of a process can be learnt from and tweaked to ensure that next time it can be done slightly better. Every iteration of a process can be measured and set gradually increasing performance goals. Although the comparison with true process management has its limits, measurement and continuous improvement can be done with change management as well.

In the situation of most organisations where there is a finite amount of resources, but a seemingly infinite variety of changes, it is necessary to put a governance process in place. Governance processes help select what changes are to be undertaken and assign a priority relative to other work in the organisation which directly determines how quickly the change can be done. Governance starts with the output from strategy development describing what the organisation exists to do and broadly identifying how this is to be achieved. Governance continues on through the mechanics of managers agreeing priorities for the specific changes, and ends with assessments of whether the chosen bundle of changes has delivered the complete objectives of the organisation.

The way an organisation is designed should take consideration of change. If you know you are going to be changing something regularly then the component you are changing can be designed to be changed regularly. Every component of an organisation can be made more or less flexible and easy to change. This can seem a little abstract, and is better understood by examples. In the telecommunications industry prices and products have to be amended all the time, so billing systems are now designed to ease this change. What once required specialist IT skills and time to amend is now a simple parameter that can be quickly changed by a less technically skilled member of staff. In manufacturing, contract manufacturers have sprung up which have production lines that can be reconfigured easily and rapidly for completely different products. In fashion retailing, some of the most successful shops are those that change their ranges very quickly, and are supported by an infrastructure that is designed to enable this change. In all of these examples core parts of an organisation have been deliberately designed with flexibility in mind.

The step-by-step guide
STEP 9 – Prepare for future changes

Step 9.1 Review and learn from this change

Part of the value of any change, and it is usually a big but unmeasured component of the benefits, is how the individual, team and organisation have grown and learnt through the process of changing. Change can be very tough and demanding, and not everything that was planned will have worked as intended. This is an ideal environment for both personal and organisational growth. One key component of good change management disciplines is to ensure the organisation learns from the experience.

Learning should not be left to accident. Of course people will learn simply by doing, but they will not necessarily optimise their learning. The way to optimise learning is by deliberately reviewing what happened in the change initiative, and taking actions to ensure that whatever can be learnt from this is learnt and is embedded into the way the organisation works.

A good and very simple way to review any project or change is to ask yourself three straightforward questions based on the concept of what should start, stop and continue:

- What was not done during this change that you should do in future? (Start)
- What went badly during this change that you should make sure you do not do in future? (Stop)
- What went well during this change that you should make sure you always do in future? (Continue)

In doing this type of review it is easy to focus on the negatives, so make sure that you also focus on the positives. It is as important to repeat what was done well as to avoid mistakes.

There is nothing new about reviewing results from a project, but too often reviews end with good intentions and limited lasting learning and development. So, having performed such a review do not stop at simply understanding what should be learnt, but drive real tangible action to ensure the knowledge is really learnt. The actions will be unique to your situation, but you can identify them by asking yourself questions like:

- How will you ensure you start, stop and continue the points you have identified?
- How will you ensure that this learning is captured and shared more widely within the organisation, so that not only you and the change team learn, but the whole organisation does?
- Do you need to adapt or enhance any of the processes, procedures or methods used for change management in the organisation? If so, how will you communicate these to the whole organisation?
- Do you need to adapt or enhance any of the roles and responsibilities used during change situations? If so, how will you do this and ensure it happens next time?
- Would your change be better supported by new systems and tools? If so, what are they and how will you ensure your organisation has access to them?
- Did anyone perform particularly well on this change? How will you ensure that the individual(s) is (are) rewarded and encouraged to repeat this behaviour on the next change and encourage it in others? How can you use this person's skills to teach others?
- Who is going to perform all the actions identified and by when? Who will ensure the action is done?

Step 9.2 Identify next change(s)

When a major change programme is complete you should be able to breathe a sigh of relief and take a short rest. However, it will only be a short rest as there will always be the next change to work on. If you came into a change team as a temporary measure from your normal work, and performed well, you may start to find that you are more valued for your ability to support successful change than for your usual role.

In all organisations there is a finite amount of project resources, and a seemingly infinite range of change projects to do. This is one example of the well-understood phenomenon of modern organisations – there is simply too much work to do. When there is too much work to do, one solution is to find extra resources. At best this is a partial solution. When you increase resources you may be able to do more, but you will also find even more to do!

The answer to this is to develop robust governance processes which help you to decide what to do, and to ensure that what you want to do is what you actually do. Governance processes are linked to your resource allocation and management approach. The whole area of resource management and optimising your available money and skills to the amount of work you do is complex and can require specialist skills and tools to deliver. However, the basic principles are not, and there are five fundamental activities:

- *Understand your resources*: how much money or budget do you have available to drive change, and how many people do you have available to work on the changes? This can be complex information to collect and assess. Essentially, you want to determine broadly how much capacity for change-related work you have.

- *Understand your possible workload*: this is effectively a list of all the possible changes you may want to make, some rough idea of how many resources they will consume, and what benefit they will provide to the organisation. In creating such a list you should include any gaps or mistakes in previous change initiatives that you now want to close.

- *Agree what criteria you will use to select and prioritise work*: what is important to your organisation? If it is profit and customer satisfaction then you should use the potential profit and customer satisfaction increases to measure and compare different change initiatives. If it is minimising staff turnover then you should use measures of staff turnover to choose between different change projects.

- *Decide between options and thin out the work*: the next activity is to thin down the list of possible change ideas from everything you might do to a list of what you will do. This will partially come from the direction set by organisational strategy, but strategy alone will not typically go to the level of detail to decide which individual projects should be undertaken and which rejected. Managers must take time to review different change initiatives and select between them.

- *Prioritise between the options you have left*: finally, decide in what order you want to do the changes. Prioritisation can be demanding and tedious, but it is important. It is very easy to start 100 change initiatives in parallel when you only have resources for 10. This will simply mean you take ages to complete anything. It is much better to start only 10, complete them quickly and then move on to the next 10. But this requires real discipline in decision making.

This simple set of activities hides a huge amount of complexity that would probably take several books to explain in any detail. For prioritisation to be effective and to be taken seriously by the whole organisation, it has to involve the most senior managers. After all, setting your change agenda equals setting the organisation's agenda for the future.

Step 9.3 Prepare for continuous change

There is continuous pressure to enhance performance, both at an individual and organisational level. The breadth of creativity and evolving capabilities across whatever sector your organisation operates in means there will always be new opportunities and new threats. The response to this must be that your organisation is always prepared to adapt and move forward. Preparation for continuous change includes:

- Developing your change management skills.
- Building flexibility into your organisation.
- Accepting that adopting change management is a change in its own right.

This capability development should start by simply instilling the expectation of ongoing change into every member of staff from the new joiner to the most experienced and longest serving member of your teams.

Whatever they are doing now will probably not be what they are required to do in future. Change must be seen as core to everyone's role, and not something special or different or that only occurs periodically. Individual change projects may end, but change itself does not. Staff must understand that every change project that successfully reaches its conclusion and is celebrated is just a stage in a never ending process. When the celebration is over, change carries on.

Building a competency in change management should be considered as a change in its own right, altering a static organisation that occasionally handles change to become a dynamic organisation that can rapidly restructure itself whenever it needs to. Factors in developing this capability include:

- Building the competencies and skills in your organisation. How many staff have good change management skills, how many do you need and how will you bridge the gap?

- Encouraging team work and cross-functional viewpoints. Change has no respect for the artificial boundaries that are designed into organisations and effective change management requires the ability to work in teams across functions. Can you currently drive change easily in a consistent way across organisational boundaries?

- Developing a capability to assess the impact of change. Good change management takes account of the impact and risk of change in any area and works to manage this impact. To do this efficiently and effectively requires a skill in risk and impact assessment. Such skills are supported by defined impact assessment processes and allocated resources to do it. Every team in your organisation needs to be ready to respond to changes thrown at them. When changes arise, how do you currently know what the impact will be on different departments?

- Developing active listening skills. Identifying the best changes to undertake, implementing them well, and understanding the response of the organisation are assisted greatly by good listening skills. Do people in your organisation listen well? If not, how are you going to ensure that they do?

- Empowering staff to take actions. Many small changes do not require the overhead of a change project, or the delay in waiting for such a project to be authorised and started. Empower your staff to make minor modifications in parts of the work under their control. Not all change needs the overhead of projects or task forces; the total quality management movement has shown how much can be achieved by allowing staff to improve their own processes and tools.

- Building reward and performance metrics around ability to deliver change successfully. Promote your high fliers from those who can deliver change, so people will value working on change. No manager of any seniority should be selected without at least some change management competence.

- Giving all managers skills to help staff with change. Not all managers are naturally adept at helping staff in change situations, at communicating the rationale for change, at motivating staff to make change, at carefully listening to staff and helping them understand the benefits of change, and where appropriate modifying change as a response to staff needs. This competency needs to be valued and developed in your managers.

It is far easier to change something that is inherently flexible than something that is not. A toy like Lego has been designed so it can be constantly reconfigured into new models, whether it is a house, a car, a machine, or a monster from a child's imagination. Organisations are built up of components such as IT systems, buildings and processes. These can be designed to be perfect at a point in time, or like Lego they can be designed with flexibility in mind in the first place. When organisations deliberately choose flexibility as a core requirement in everything they develop, then when the time comes to change this it is easier. Almost every facet of an organisation can be built with flexibility in mind, for example:

- *People*: when you recruit do you select the best people for a role, or do you choose people who have the best capability to deliver value to your organisation in a situation in which their roles will continually change? Do you write contracts and job specifications that are very specific to a role or are they written in the expectation that they will change?

- *IT systems*: do you design and build your IT systems with consideration of the functionality and data you require today, or do you know that this will change and so design IT systems that are easy to modify?

- *Buildings*: do you have buildings that suit your precise organisational structure right now, or are they configured so you can move people around as the organisation changes?

- *Machinery*: is the machinery you buy easy to change as your products evolve or will it only work precisely for today's products?

- *Logistics and supply chain*: is your supply chain designed to be as efficient as possible for today's issues, or have you considered how you can have flexibility in supply as your demands change?

- *Business processes*: are your processes clearly documented and maintained so that if there is requirement to change them you understand what you are changing? If they are documented, do the documents represent what should or could happen – or do they really represent what does happen?

- *Product, services and prices*: if you need to make a modification to any part of the product or services your organisation provides can you do this rapidly with minimal overhead or is it a nightmare each time? Are your products and services built from flexible components that can be rapidly reconfigured without need for a change project or development work?

In each situation there will be a cost of flexibility, and in some cases you may choose not to develop flexibility if the cost is too high. However, flexibility should be a real consideration in the design and development of every component of your organisation.

The final factor to consider is that applying change management is a change in its own right. Methodologies such as Six Sigma emphasise that they are as much about changing the way you work as about delivering any one specific change. Change management is not an add-on skill that you require now and again – it is one of the core management skills required. Organisations that are adept at change management think and operate differently to those that are not. If you have not done it already, one of the first change programmes you may want to consider is the embedding of change management into the everyday way of working.

Key tips

- Every change provides an opportunity to learn. True learning is not just about discussing what went well and badly, but about taking real action to ensure the lessons are drilled into the organisation.

- Change is continuous in an environment of finite resources. To perform the best changes requires tough decision making and prioritisation of change options.

- To thrive in a world of change your organisation should deliberately develop change management skills as a core skill for everyone in the organisation.

- When you are developing or changing anything in your organisation consider how you can design in flexibility so the next time it comes to making a modification it is easier, quicker and cheaper.

TO DO NOW

- Think through how you will review and learn from your latest change – did you do it well? Do you think the organisation as a whole has learnt from the change? What is the most important lesson that has been learnt? What should have been learnt, but probably has not been?

- Decide what you are going to do next to enhance your change management skills.

- Consider where flexibility can be built into your organisation. How will this ease change in future? Do you think this is worth doing?

- Decide what your next change will be!

Conclusion

Now you have completed *Managing Change: Step by Step*, then if you follow the steps in this book, applying relevant judgement and understanding of your situation, you should be able to implement a wide range of changes.

You started in step 1 by building up your vocabulary and understanding of simple change management concepts. Then in step 2 you learnt how to define clearly the objective of a change, and decide how you will reach this objective. In step 3 you built your change team. By following the activities in step 4 you will have designed your change in detail. In step 5 you reviewed the levels of support and resistance to the change and thought through how to overcome these, and in step 6 you started to implement the change. Having implemented the change, in step 7 you made sure that the benefits of the change were really built into your organisation. Working alongside all of this, you followed the activities in step 8 to ensure that all the communications required were carried out. Finally, in this step you reviewed where you go next to build change skills into your organisation.

What's next? Change should not be viewed as an individual event but as a constant series of activities. Change is a conveyor belt, not a once-off situation. Change management challenges continually expand, and the discipline does as well. Change management is not just a part of your organisation's skill set, but a core part of it.

I will leave you with a final thought to contemplate. In some organisations the constant honing and enhancing of skills in change management is so important that they enforce some change even though it may not be necessary at a specific point in time. The logic is that, like an athlete in training between competitions, or a soldier exercising on manoeuvres during peace time, change capabilities are so essential to an organisation that they have to be maintained and developed all the time. I have mixed feelings about this approach – but now you have read this step-by-step guide to change, you have to start to make your own decisions about issues like this.

Good luck, whatever your decision is!

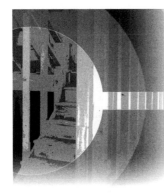

Appendix

Adapting the step-by-step approach

Adapting the step-by-step approach	**A.1** Assess the characteristics of the change
	A.2 Identify other unique techniques
	A.3 Review the role of the whole management community
	A.4 Adapt when you build your change team
	A.5 Modify your way of planning

THIS APPENDIX PROVIDES:

- A variety of optional guidance to help you review the nature of the change you are making, the environment in which you are working, and using this information to decide how to modify the approach to managing your change.

THE CENTRAL POINT IS:

- There is not one type of change, and there is not a single way to approach change. Change management methodologies are only helpful if they are applicable both to the change you want to make and the environment in which you work. The approach you take to change must be tailored depending on the nature of the change you are making and the character of your organisation.

Setting the scene

To help understand the need to adapt your approach to change depending on the situation, consider three very typical changes that different organisations often undertake:

1. To develop and install a new IT system to manage customer orders in a nationwide company. This was previously done manually. By automating order processing the business hopes to reduce the level of errors and the cost of order processing.

2. To identify and remove costs from a business as a result of huge losses. The losses have generated a need to improve profitability rapidly, otherwise the business will go bankrupt.

3. For a government organisation providing services to the general public to respond to the macro-level trends in society and hence demands on the organisation. This has identified the need generally to improve the technical and management skills and the customer focus of the staff in the organisation. Many people in the organisation do not understand the need for this change, and there is a risk they may actively oppose it, or passively resist simply by ignoring it.

The IT systems change is straightforward to understand and specify. If managed well, delivery of this type of change will be typified by a well-structured, planned project which will take a known amount of time and cost a known amount of money. IT projects can be very complex and demanding, but much of the complexity of development of an IT system comes in truly understanding user requirements, followed by the technical development of the software. There is a change management element to the work, and many IT projects fail because of poor change management. However, with some clear thinking and planning it is easy to determine that the staff in order processing will have to prepare for and train on the new system, and business processes will need to be adapted to activities now done by the system rather than manually. In terms of approach, this change is best handled as a project with a very clear end goal – a fully implemented computer system, supported by applying change management as the system is put in place.

The second change is different. The end goal is arguably even clearer – reduced costs are absolute, whereas a good computer system is a subjective judgement. However, the way to get to this end goal, and to measure it in real life, is less immediately apparent and there are many options to pursue. Given that there is a risk that the business involved will become bankrupt unless costs are reduced quickly, there is a real urgency to get the work done. At the start of the work it is not possible to predict how long it will take and how much cost will be saved. No stone can be left unturned in looking for costs to cut out of the business. In some situations there will be a need for sensitivity, perhaps even secrecy, as some people may need to be made redundant. Although many people will dislike the changes made, given that the alternative may be to go bankrupt, any resistance is likely to be minimal. Unlike the development of a computer system, such cost-cutting work will not be a discrete project, separate from the day-to-day running of the business, but it will be the core item in everyone's daily work. New rules may have to be agreed and quickly put in place, for example to reduce staff expenses and to limit buying to the most essential supplies. Everyone in the business must immediately understand the need to avoid unnecessary expenditure and to look for costs to reduce. The initiative may result in some projects being started to reduce costs, but completing any one project will not be enough.

The third change is the most difficult to define precisely. An organisation knows when a computer system is in place, and with adequate financial controls would know when cost cutting had gone far enough to bring it back into profit, but when are there enough skills or the right attitude in an organisation? This type of change will almost certainly take longer, perhaps several years, as enhancing skills and attitudes takes time. It is a more pervasive change, complex to communicate and keep control of. When the objective is communicated in terms of improved skills and attitudes, or enhanced culture, different individuals will almost certainly interpret it in alternative ways and approach the change in an inconsistent manner. There is limited immediate urgency as this is more about building the right capabilities in an organisation for the future than solving a short-term problem. Gaining acceptance for the need for such a change when there is no current problem can be very hard. Much of the work will be about communicating the skills and attitudes required, for senior managers to model the behaviour they want to see, and to reward those acting in that way. It is more about adapting behaviour than planned steps in a project. It will require changes to the performance management system in the organisation, so those with the skills wanted and displaying the desired attitudes to work get the maximum rewards. Achievement of the objective will be at least partially determined by management judgement as by a clear-cut measure. Facing a challenge like this is very different from either the first or the second situation.

Introduction to the key characteristics of change

The steps in this book provided a generic approach to successfully managing change. It is important to realise that the approach must be tweaked to the type of change you are making. This appendix provides some thoughts to help you adapt the change approach to the specific situation you are in. Applying this guidance requires judgement. This appendix does not contain precise rules, but a series of points to reflect on. In reflecting you have to make your own judgements about how best to approach your situation. Understanding this appendix will help you to emphasise certain parts of the change management process, whilst reducing the focus on others.

One way this is achieved is to consider the characteristics of the change you are undertaking. The guidance in step A.1 reviews some characteristics of change that I have found need to be taken into account when deciding on your approach. The guidance in step A.2 is more generic and is intended to stimulate your own thinking about your change and to determine if there is anything you can identify which is unique or different about your change. Having performed steps A.1 and A.2, you will have a better understanding of the uniqueness of your change.

The remainder of this appendix looks at some specific areas you may need to modify your approach in three areas: how the general managers in the business should be involved in the change, when to pull the change team together, and how to plan your change. Although this appendix is structured in the same way as the main chapters of the book, the steps here should not be considered as a process to follow in the order they are written, but as additional material to take into consideration when planning your change. In reality any steps in the process described in this book may need adaptation for specific changes. The points identified in this appendix are just some common areas for review.

The step-by-step guide APPENDIX – Adapting the step-by-step approach

Step A.1 Assess the characteristics of the change

Table A.1 describes 14 characteristics of change to think about. The information in the table is split into three columns. The first column describes a typical characteristic of a change project. The second column provides some sample questions to ask yourself to understand your change relative to this characteristic. The final column explains the influence of this characteristic upon your change, and indicates how your could tailor your approach depending on this characteristic.

Whilst some situations are easier to deal with than others, there is no right or wrong answers with these characteristics. Change has to occur in whatever situation the organisation is changing, and as a change management professional you have to learn to deal with different situations by adapting your approach. The 14 characteristics are not an exhaustive list of considerations, but some areas I have personally had to deal regularly with.

This table does not give answers, but should trigger your own thinking to provide answers relevant to your situation. By reading through these characteristics you will become more aware of the nature of your change or the environment in which you operate and from this be able to make decisions about how to modify your approach.

Overview	Questions	Explanation and impact on change approach
	Understanding and acceptance of rationale for change	
In step 2 of this book (understand your objective), you defined the objective for your change. Unfortunately, just because you have an objective does not mean that everyone you work with understands and agrees with it. The first characteristic of your change to consider is therefore how well the rationale for change is understood, and how widely it is accepted	Is there generally support and understanding in your organisation for the objective you are trying to achieve? How well is the rationale for change understood and accepted in your organisation? Who does not support your objective and what is the likely effect of this?	Where there is common support for an objective you do not need to take any specific action, and you have a good basis for moving forward with your change. However, there will not always be common agreement. Consider the situation of a business that is set up as a partnership with two partners. One partner is extremely ambitious, and wants to grow the business to be a major company. The other partner is happy with the business as it is, as it generates enough income and enables him to maintain the work life balance he wants. To grow the business both partners should agree to the objective. Hence time will have to be spent at the beginning of the change developing a level of consensus between the partners as to the ideal level of growth. Sometimes a disagreement over objectives cannot be resolved by consensus and other action must be taken, for example one partner could buy the other out; or if one partner is more senior he or she could simply overrule the other, but the other partner may still resist. Either way, effort must be spent determining how to move forward with the objective you have, and managing the impact of the approach you determine.

Change is easier when there is consensus on, and a common understanding of, your objective. If these do not exist you will have to spend time and effort gaining them. Alternatively, if consensus is not possible and compromise is not appropriate, you will have to use logical and emotional argument, influence and power to ensure that those who disagree with the change do not adversely inhibit its progress.

In these situations you must allocate extra time to achieve the appropriate outcome.

Understanding and acceptance of proposed change

Even when you have reached agreement on your objective, it does not mean you have agreement on how to achieve this objective. The change you are making may be only one way to achieve an objective. Other staff may consider alternative changes as better ways to realise your objective. A common situation in which this occurs is between unions and management in businesses. Both may accept that change needs to be made, but they may have opposing views about the most appropriate change to make.	Are there perceived to be alternative ways to achieve your change objective? Are you convinced that the approach you have selected is best? Why? Is there generally support and understanding in your organisation for the proposed approach and consensus that your currently chosen solution is the most appropriate way to achieve your objective? How will you convince others that the approach you have chosen is the best?	Two senior managers in a business may both agree with an objective such as the business should achieve a growth rate of at least 10%, but they may strongly disagree about how best to achieve this. Each manager could have their own idea as to how best to grow the business. In some situations such a disagreement will not be a problem as organisations often have to try many solutions at once to achieve an objective, and perhaps these senior managers will agree to try to implement both of their preferred approaches to achieve growth. However, there will always be finite resources available to deliver changes. Where there is not enough resources, one or other solution must be chosen as the preferred approach.

Overview	Questions	Explanation and impact on change approach
	Understanding and acceptance of proposed change	
		Gaining agreement about which way to achieve an objective can be done by more analysis, detailed business cases and ongoing debate. This, however, takes time and effort, time that you may want to be spending implementing your change rather than discussing it. The more options there are, and the more disagreement about what is the best option, the more time you are likely to spend in this initial business case phase.
	Type of change – hard or soft	
One way to think about the nature of a change is on a spectrum from hard to soft. Hard in this context is a reference not to how difficult the change is, but to how tangible and definable the end result is. Soft changes are those in which the end result is more nebulous and difficult to define and measure precisely. An example of a hard change is to build a series of new offices to provide accommodation for 1,000 staff. An example of a soft change is to change an organisational culture to be more forward thinking and open to customer feedback.	Is this a very clear change that will take a fixed amount of time, has understood deliverables and with little emotional impact on people? Or is it an open-ended change where it is not possible to clearly predict the end point and which is the core impact on people's attitudes? Is the initiative you are proposing a pure project with tangible deliverables or is it about changing people?	Hard changes are more likely to be successful when managed by applying a project management approach with some consideration of change management given. Soft changes cannot be achieved by simply planning and delivering a project, but need to bring a broad range of interpersonal, relationship management and communication skills to bear. Hard changes can usually be easily and clearly communicated to an organisation, whereas great care needs to be taken over soft changes as ambiguity is often difficult to avoid.

Alternatively, a hard change can be specified in terms of a clear and unambiguous measure, such as a financial target, whereas soft changes usually have to be measured indirectly.

Type of change – deliverable or goal

Another related way to consider a change is if it is defined in terms of the creation of a deliverable or in terms of achieving a goal. This may seem like semantics, and there is not an absolute boundary between the two, but it is an important difference.	Is your change defined in terms of the creation of some deliverables or in terms of the achievement of a specific performance objective? Is there a clear task (or set of tasks) that when completed will mean you have completed your change? Can your change be described in terms of a project or is it more an area of performance to focus on?	The chief executive made an announcement to all staff in the organisation. As part of the improvement in working conditions all staff will be moved to a new purpose-built facility about 750 m away. This was part of a wider initiative to improve staff satisfaction. In this case the selection, fitting and move of all staff to a new facility is a project. The overall initiative to improve staff satisfaction is not a project as it does not have a specific end point. It will be achieved by a series of projects and ongoing management attention. [This is described in more detail in step A.3 below]

▶

Overview	Questions	Explanation and impact on change approach
	Boundary of change	
When you make a change it has a resultant impact upon people in the organisation. This impact may be very local or alternatively can be very broad, and affect a large number of people. The boundary of change defines the limits to the impact of a change.	Do you know who will be affected by this change? Does this change affect only a specific bounded group of people all under the control of the change team, or are the boundaries wider, vaguer or with the possibility of impact on a very large group of people who may have nothing to do with the change? Will the change affect people external to your organisation, and how will you prepare them for the change?	If a change only affects a limited group of people in one department and you are their line manager, ensuring the change is successful is far easier than when the impact of a change extends more widely across an organisation or to stakeholders external to the organisation. For an extreme example of a change with very wide boundaries, consider the contentious situation of the compulsory addition of additives to certain food types for perceived health benefits. No matter how much the originators of such change believe this is the right thing to do, they will face a struggle convincing some proportion of the general public. Obviously, a government can simply mandate such a change, as it has done in a few situations, but in doing so it risks bad feelings and can alienate a group of its own supporters. These people may turn into a very vocal and energetic opposition to the change. Such changes take significant time and money to communicate widely in trying to influence people's attitudes to support the change. When you have an open boundary to your change you must consider how you will assess and react to the views and actions of those beyond your control and influence.

Risk associated with change failure

Every change you take has a risk associated with it. The end result of change is not completely predictable and there is a risk that the change may fail.

In some situations the chance of change failure is minimal. In other changes, especially with experimental modifications, or transformations into new unfamiliar areas, the risk of failure is higher. The issue is not simply the likelihood of change failure, though, but what the impact on your organisation is, if failure occurs.

What will happen if the change fails?

What is the likelihood of change failure?

If the change fails could you or the change team manage the outcome?

What is the appropriate level of management to authorise taking such a risk?

What can you do to reduce this risk?

The least that can happen if a change project fails is that the investment in the change is wasted. Depending on how much time and money has been invested, this may be completely irrelevant or a problem for the managers who are driving the change. At the other extreme, the risk to organisations from some change failures can be complete organisational collapse. If your change is at the extreme end of risk then your risk management needs to be very strong, and you will need to ensure you have the full support of key stakeholders such as the organisation's owners. If you are literally risking the survival of an organisation through a change then you need to be very confident you are getting it right. For example, when some construction projects fail, because of the scale of investment involved, the building companies will go bankrupt. When a telecoms company changes its billing and customer care systems, if the initiative fails the impact on customers can be catastrophic. When a car manufacturer invests in a new model, if the car is unpopular the implications for the company can be huge. On the other hand, if your change is to add a new field to an order form, then the risk of error and impact if it happens is small.

Overview	Questions	Explanation and impact on change approach
	Risk associated with change failure	
		There are several approaches to managing and reducing risk, but they all start by understanding what your level of risk is. In high-risk situations when it comes to implementing the change, the way you trial, test and pilot the change will be of paramount importance. Hence the proportion of time and resources allocated to testing, customer or staff trials, and other activities associated with proving a solution, will be larger.
	Origin of driver for change	
As discussed in step 1 (learn the basics), changes may originate within an organisation or may be thrust upon it by external pressure (either in the general environment in which the organisation operates or because of pressure of influential external stakeholders).	Is the change internally driven or externally driven? Is the change something the organisation is driving or merely responding to? How much control do you have over the change?	Where a change is truly internally driven an organisation has the luxury of planning the change in detail and making sure preparations are fully in place. At the other extreme when changes are forced upon an organisation, there is not always the ability to control the timing or the plans. You must simply respond to someone else's instructions. Irrespective of how important or risky a change is, when it is forced from outside the pace of change is often faster than an organisation would choose itself and a change project may have to be more reactive than proactive.

Urgency for change

In some situations there is an obvious and universally understood immediate need for change; in others there is less compelling instant need and potentially even less consensus about the need altogether.

Is there an absolute or obvious urgent need for the change (e.g. a business will go bankrupt unless it happens now), or is there less immediate pressure with the change being more about longer term issues?

What will happen if you leave the change for a while and do it later?

How much time can you delay the change for without problems – a day, a week, a month, a year or longer?

How can you generate a sense of urgency for your change?

If there is a clear and obvious need for change it is far easier to get people's agreement to and support for a change. Taking an extreme example, when a block of flats is burning down it does not take much effort to convince people to leave the building.

Typically, the higher the sense of need altogether urgency for change, the easier it is to overcome any barriers to change.

On the other hand, where the need to make change is less compelling, especially if it is less immediately obvious that it is essential and can be delayed for more time, it takes much more effort to convince people about the change. If the block of flats is not burning down but in need of redecoration, it may take time to convince all residents to vacate their premises to allow the decorating to take place. They may not even agree it needs decoration or feel it can be delayed for another few months or even years. Urgency is so helpful to change that some change management experts even suggest artificially creating a sense of urgency if it is not there naturally. With the block of flats, a sense of urgency might be achieved by telling residents that their flats will be worth less if they are not decorated, and that painting will increase values significantly, or more deviously saying that the flats are dangerous and need some work to make them safe.

▶

Overview	Questions	Explanation and impact on change approach
Level of support for change in general		
Different groups of people have different innate attitudes towards change. Some groups are open to change. They may agree or disagree with a specific change initiative, but they have a history of responding flexibly. Other groups may be very conservative, and almost irrespective of the change may resist adaptation. The fear of the new and resistance against change in general are very common.	Does the organisation in which you are working have a track record in welcoming or resisting change? Do you consider the staff and management as flexible and adaptable or rigid and inflexible? Can you make changes freely or do you have powerful stakeholders, such as shareholders and unions, you need to convince first?	It is easier to work with flexible organisations with staff who have a history of change. Partly this will be because of the skills they have built up. Also it is because they do not find change, in itself, to be emotional or threatening as they are wrenched from a current way of working to a new way. Very conservative organisations often have to start by changing only small areas to get people used to the concept of change. Change management professionals tend to consider that they are personally very open to change. If you want to test your own level of openness to change, think about when you go into a supermarket and find it has rearranged the position of goods on shelves around the shop. Do you think of it as an interesting innovation, or as an irritating tinkering with something that already worked? Essentially, it typically takes more effort to get conservative organisations to change, and ongoing work to keep the change project moving.
Degree of organisational readiness for this change		
In some situations an organisation, whether or not a change is welcome, is ready and waiting	Will this change come as a surprise, or is this organisation ready for it? Will individual staff be taken aback when the	Surprise about change is usually a bad thing. Surprise may even come about when changes are being made that are not a secret, if they are being done sooner than expected, or if the

for a specific alteration; in others the modifications will come as a surprise.

change is announced or will it be something they are prepared for?

concept of change was known, but no one really believed it would happen. When people are surprised they are less likely to be open to change, respond badly, or at least to respond without thinking clearly. Many labour disputes have been caused by trying to force change that has come as a surprise to staff. In some situations change is deliberately brought in as a surprise, because it is felt that the change will cause disruption anyway and this can be best managed when the change team is ready. This sometimes works, but it is a risky approach. If you are working towards an expected change, even if people do not like it, they will tend to be prepared or resigned to it, and their energies will be focused on making the best of it. People most actively try to disrupt change they both do not like and are surprised by. They can even fight against change that they later come to admire. The level of readiness will therefore directly impact the work you have to do.

Level of change skills, competencies and experience

Many organisations have recognised the need for change management, and because they are in very rapidly changing environments have built up a wide range of experience and skills in

Do you have a wide pool of resource with relevant experience to work on your change? Is the organisation used to change? Is there an understanding and expectation of what change and change management mean? Where will you find the people you need in your change team?

As an early part of the change you will need to determine where you will gain access to the necessary change management skills and competencies. If you are lucky you will have a pool of skilled resources to choose from, often you will not. The solution to the problem of too few resources may include training

Overview	Questions	Explanation and impact on change approach
Level of change skills, competencies and experience		
handling change. Other organisations, especially those which have traditionally operated in a much more stable environment, may have very limited existing change skills.		existing staff, recruiting new staff to act as role models or subject matter experts in change, or making use of consultants and contractors. This will affect the time it takes to get your change started. Fewer skills tend to heighten the risk that something will go wrong that could have been avoided. If you use external consultants, the cost of your change initiative will usually increase.
Degree of openness possible		
There are many situations in organisations in which decisions are made in secret amongst a small group of senior managers. This may be because openness is not possible (you should differentiate between a desire to remain secret and a real need to work in secrecy).	Can you be open about your intentions, or are there legal, regulatory, financial, ethical or other practical reasons why you must keep silent about the change? If you must develop a change in secret, how and when will you communicate? What will the resultant response be? How will you manage this?	If your proposed change has to remain secret until the time it is fully implemented then you cannot rely on communicating and other activities to gain buy-in and support for the change. You may need to do more communicating after the change to explain what could not be explained before. The change will come as a surprise, and, as previously noted, this is likely to affect adversely the response to the change.
Degree of openness possible		
Whenever possible secrecy should be avoided, as sooner or later what you are doing will become apparent and this can result in very strong negative		Additionally, you are likely to have a much more limited pool of resources to work on the change. If an activity is to remain secret then in practice you can only work with a small number of people (otherwise who are you keeping it secret

emotions and actions. However, there are both optimal and sub-optimal times for openness, and there are some situations in which you must retain secrecy. There are, for example, rules and regulations about how you communicate certain financial transactions such as mergers and takeovers. Also, for practical reasons, if you are making a large number of staff redundant you will want to control how and when you tell them. Again there are also guidelines and rules about how such communications must be made, and if you work closely with partners such as trade unions you may have agreed formal processes for such communications, which means you must retain confidentiality until you have followed the agreed process.

from?). If you do have to have a large change team then you must be responsive to leaks of confidential material, and ensure that the change team is prohibited from telling anyone else about the change. One way to do this is by getting people to sign an NDA (Non-Disclosure Agreement) for the life of the change. Such documents are effectively contracts to keep a secret, which can be helpful in retaining confidentiality, but for the largest of teams are unlikely to be foolproof.

Overview	Questions	Explanation and impact on change approach
Type of measure of success for change		
Sometimes a change is driven to achieve a clear and single measure of success such as a financial improvement in the state of an enterprise. Often, though, this has to be factored against other measures (or constraints), such as customer and staff satisfaction.	Are the measures straightforward financial measures, or are they softer measures? Is there one dimension to success or many? Is your change initiative being measured against short-term or long-term benefits? Are the measures used true measures of what you want to achieve? If not, how will you ensure you get the result you want? Are your measures likely to drive any behaviour you do not want, and if so how will you manage this?	There is rarely, truly, only a single dimension to change. Where there are multiple factors trading off against each other, such as in a cost-reduction initiative retaining high staff satisfaction, at some point these two measures of success will conflict. You must prepare a mechanism to enable trade-offs between the various measures and decide which compromises are best. Your steering committee is a good place to make such decisions. If you are working to achieve longer term benefits, how will you measure them and how will you know when to stop your change project if the full benefits have not yet been achieved? The more complex and multidimensional your success criteria, the more complex your decision-making and governance processes will be.
Change environment/number of parallel changes		
You may be lucky enough to work in an organisation in which the change you wish to make is the only change happening to the affected group of people. More commonly in modern organisations, the change you are working on is only one of a plethora of changes happening in parallel.	Is this change the only modification ongoing in your organisation, or are there many separate changes happening in parallel? Do any of the parallel changes affect the same group of people as your change? Do any of the parallel changes affect your ability to complete the change you are trying to implement?	Where multiple changes are happening in parallel you will have to contend for resources to be allocated to your change initiative, and you will also be in competition for people's attention when you communicate the change. Additionally, understanding how people will respond to a change is not possible without some knowledge of what else is happening to them.

How do you know and assess the total set of changes your organisation is undergoing?		A change project to upgrade all the PCs in core offices of a university sounds straightforward, and should, on its own, pose few difficult challenges. But if it occurs when people are extremely busy working on and responding to other changes, such as introducing a new type of exam, changing the profile of students at the university, and altering the funding regime, the staff will have less capacity to learn about the new computers and far less tolerance of the time lost when their own PC is being exchanged. Appreciation of cumulative change from the viewpoint of the people being changed is essential for good change management. The change manager has to be able to see the change from the viewpoint of the community being changed, and if they are undergoing many other changes in parallel this will affect their speed and capability to adapt to the change.

Complexity, scale and length of change initiative

Some small procedural changes may be planned and implemented in a few days, whereas large-scale cultural programmes and business	Is your change small and discrete, or is it of a large-scale cutting across many functions and taking a long time to implement? Is the budget for this change within your own level of authorisation, or do you need other	A very large and complex change will require a significantly higher degree of planning and management skills to deliver. A large change will require more time and effort to gain approval for the investment in the change. A small change

▶

Overview	Questions	Explanation and impact on change approach
Complexity, scale and length of change initiative		
transformations can take months and years. Some changes do not require any additional budget beyond a department's existing budget; others will need many millions of pounds of extra funding to be allocated to them.	levels of authorisation? How used to this scale of change is your organisation and how long will it take to gain authorisation? Do you have all the resources avaliable for the scale of change you envisage? Will the team which starts the change see it to completion?	can be paid for from a manager's own budget and probably approved by that manager. Very large changes need extra funds, and will need the approval of senior managers and even external stakeholders such as shareholders (or the government or trustees for public bodies). Tracking progress in a small change can be done by a line manager as part of normal work, but tracking progress and proving success for a large change can be highly complex. The team on a small change project will normally complete the change, whereas a large change taking many months or even years may have to cope with turnover of staff in the change team.

Table A.1 Common change characteristics

Step A.2 Identify other unique features

Step A.1 looked at some of the common variable characteristics of many change initiatives that I have come across. However, no list of characteristics can cover all the unique features of every possible change. When planning your change you should ask yourself – is there anything else different or special about your change?

To help you think this through, here are some change scenarios that have unique characteristics. The specific situations can be accounted for in the way change is managed:

- Merging two departments in a multinational company which will result in the consolidation of a French and a Chinese team into a single department under a single American manager. How would you cope with the language barriers and cultural differences?

- Opening up a women's educational institute to men. As well as emotional and political issues, there may be practical barriers to overcome. Does this pose any specific challenge?

- Moving business operations to another country pwith different business practices, laws and regulations. How would you understand and assess the impact of this?

In addition, the change may be uniquely affected by things happening around it. Are there any events occurring which will impact this change? For example:

- The change must be implemented over Christmas when there will be limited staff available to do the implementation work. How would you plan for this?

- The change must be implemented and shown to be fully working at the same time as a change in health and safety regulations. How would you ensure your change is consistent with the new health and safety regulations that are not yet fully defined?

- Driving an unpopular change in a charitable organisation that works mainly with volunteers, who can cease work any time, and has a formal decision-making committee that only meets twice a year. How will you manage change with volunteers over whom you have limited formal control? How will you deal with the infrequent opportunities for decision making and approvals?

The examples described in this step are not meant to relate to any specific change you may have but to spur your own assessment of your change and any individual challenges it brings about.

Step A.3 Review the role of the whole management community

The objective of this book is to provide you with a simple way to manage changes to successful conclusions. The approach describes change being driven by an individual change manager supported by a change team. The change manager and the change team come together temporarily for the life of the change initiative, like a project team. The change team works alongside the normal management structure of the organisation, developing the change deliverables and then implementing them into the organisation. This is a great way to manage most changes. However, for very large changes a central change team, alone, will not be able to implement all the steps in this book across all parts of the organisation that are affected.

When the change in hand is a large business transformation – such as following a merger, during a radical cost-cutting programme or a cultural change programme – the change is not an additional activity outside and on top of normal operations, but a core component of every manager's role. There is usually still a need for a central change team to co-ordinate activity across the organisation, to drive progress towards the change objectives, to monitor and report at an organisational level on progress, and to measure the achievement of the benefits associated with the change. But the overall change team is the management team of the business.

Considering every manager in an organisation as part of the change team is a broad subject which is beyond the scope of a step-by-step guide like this. This section introduces the subject and provides a general awareness of the concept.

Although using the whole management community as the change team can be complex to manage, there are a number of major advantages beyond the simple and obvious one of more people to do the work. The first advantage is that the managers are much more likely to support the adoption of the change when they have been involved in its design and implementation. The second advantage is that when managers support the adoption of the change their teams are more likely to do so as well. Although we talk about organisational culture as if it is one common thing across an organisation, it is not. Every team has its own culture which is usually derived from the style of leadership, management and interaction the team manager uses. A well-motivated manager, whose team has respect for and faith in him or her, will make change happen irrespective of the response elsewhere in the organisation. If your whole management community supports the change, and are respected by their teams, then implementation is much easier.

In the situation of a major business transformation, every manager has to take responsibility for implementing the change in their team and area of management responsibility. Key activities every manager must do in relation to the change include:

- Developing a full understanding of the change.
- Modelling the change and leading the team by example. This is supported by showing passion and belief in the change.
- Assessing the impact of the change on individuals in their team, and on their team's work. Where there are multiple parallel changes, line managers are ideally placed to understand the cumulative impact on their teams.
- Determining the necessary response and actions required to manage this impact.
- Supporting the individuals in their team through the change.
- Implementing any actions required to be done by their team.
- Ensuring their team has access to any resources required to deliver the change successfully.
- Maintaining clear communication to the team about the change for the life of the change successfully .
- Maintaining communication back to the central change team on progress, issues, risks, as well as comments and ideas from their team.
- Measuring and reporting on progress towards delivering the change in their team to the central change team.
- Measuring, and striving for, adherence to the change once it has been made.

- Setting suitable performance targets for their team members which encourage adherence to the change.
- Ensuring that their team continues to do its normal job, and works towards existing organisational goals during the process of change.

Where change is a part of every manager's role, managers ideally need:

- General change management awareness and training.
- To understand fully the implications of change on their teams, and to understand how all changes fit within the overall direction and strategy of the organisation.
- To have the capability and freedom to interpret the change in the way that is most relevant to their team, whilst remaining consistent and co-ordinated with the overall change.
- Good communication skills to be able to receive ongoing communication on the change, and to be able to communicate onwards effectively to their teams.
- To see delivery of the change as part of their core role, and to have objectives set and performance management incentives defined to be consistent with this.
- To have the capability to coach staff.

Developing this range of skills and capabilities greatly strengthens an organisation. Organisations do not complete a change and then stop changing. For most organisations change can no longer be considered as a transactional activity that occurs from time to time, but must be regarded as a continuous part of the organisation's work. Hence the responsibilities defined above and the capability to exercise these responsibilities competently must become a permanent part of every manager's skill set.

Step A.4 Adapt when you build your change team

When you completed step 2 (understand your objective), you understood your proposed change: why you want to do it, what needs to be changed, and by how much. You were ready to start planning, costing and implementing your change. To implement the change you will need a team which does the work to make the change happen. Step 3 (build the change team) described all about building this change team.

As in all the steps in this book, you have to be pragmatic and apply common sense to make change work in your situation. The order of steps can be altered if that is required for your change. There is a particular chicken and egg dilemma about the order of steps 2 and 3 – you may not be able to do step 2 without having done step 3, but you should not do step 3 until you have completed step 2. Without doing step 2 first then you will not be able to direct the team selected in step 3. However, for complex changes step 2 is a lot of work and needs the change team to do.

The answer is to start step 3 when it is most appropriate. It is usually easiest to get resources allocated when there is a sense of urgency for the change. For a small change, the individual manager conceiving the change should be able to do all of step 2 and only pull a team together to implement the change once he or she fully understands the change. On the other hand, for a complex change, carrying out the activities described in steps 2.5 to 2.10, especially those related to collecting data, will require substantial effort.

So when should you start step 3? Start it too early and you may have insufficient work and direction for your change team. (It is also possible that approval for the change will be rejected and you will only have to disband the team again.) Start step 3 too late and you may end up unable to do the activities described in steps 2.5 to 2.10. You must therefore make a sensible judgement as to when to start to build your change team. There are no hard and fast rules, but if you start to find the activities in step 2.5 onwards too much work for yourself, now is the time to start working on step 3 in parallel to step 2.

The reality is that change team members will join and leave the change team at different times across the life of the change. As a change manager you must ensure you have adequate resources with the right skill set throughout the life of the change project.

Step A.5 Modify your way of planning

Step 4 (plan how to achieve change) looked at achieving a change initiative by applying the project management approach of developing a plan. The plan is based on the activities required to meet the end goal of the project. There is a related, but slightly different, way to look at change initiatives. This is the concept of using task forces with a targeted plan over 30, 60 or 90 days.

Some changes are less suitable to be considered as a project. When there is not a clearly defined set of deliverables, or when there is no one specific end point, the structure of a project will not work effectively. Projects are also not effective at delivering work which regularly and rapidly changes scope. An alternative to the project in these situations is the task force.

Task forces were described in step 1 (learn the basics). As a reminder, a task force is a group of people to which you give a bold short-term improvement goal. The goal should be well defined and limited in scope. Although the task should be limited in scope, task forces can be ve ry effective at tackling major cross-functional problems. By 'cross-functional problems' I mean problems that do not fall within a single manager's responsibility or capability to resolve. To resolve cross-functional problems managers from different functions must work together to identify and implement solutions. Good examples of the use of task forces could be to remove a backlog of customer complaints, rapidly reduce fault rates associated with a service, or fulfilling all open orders before the Christmas break. Task forces can use many of the same disciplines of a good project, such as issue and risk management, but the normal approach to planning will not work.

A great way for a task force to work is to a plan over 30, 60 or 90 days, though in this case the 'plan' is not quite the same as the plan a project manager would recognise. The plan is less about task and more about achievement or outcome. Hence a task force may have a 90-day plan to reduce customers' complaints by 90%. After 30 days it aims to have reduced them by 20%, after 60 days by 60% and after 90 days by 90%. The targets should be ambitious as they are used to create constructive challenge, drive energy and creative thinking. At the start of the project the targets are set – without necessarily knowing how they are to be achieved. The plan is therefore less a structure which is used to allocate tasks and manage progress, but more a schedule of what progress should have been achieved by certain points in time. This plan provides a basis for measuring and driving progress.

The danger of the task force mentality can be chaos, especially if there are too many task forces running in parallel without any prioritisation over their work. Also if there is too much focus on the task force's short-term goals, irrespective of long-term impact, you can end up with problems.

The answer is not to avoid planning, but to plan simply, rapidly and to revisit continuously the plan throughout the life of the task force. The difference between this approach and the planned approach described in step 4 is one of emphasis. Good task forces are energetic and they attack a problem fast. They work quickly, try solutions, measure the results and, if they have not achieved the goal, try others. They work in a controlled and structured way – just as a good project team should. Well-run task forces, for example using some Six Sigma techniques, can dramatically improve performance in relatively short periods of time.

Task forces work best for change initiatives focused on improvement to a specific performance metric. They do not work so well when a change initiative requires significant development work (such as major new systems implementation or development of new products), or when the change is longer term. They can, however, be used in conjunction with more traditional planning styles as a way to energise and kickstart a larger change programme.

References

There are literally thousands of books on change management and the supporting topics covered in this book. Here are a few that may be useful:

- One of the most influential and accessible writers on change is John Kotter. He has written a number of books on the topic which are worth reading, including:

  Leading Change, John P. Kotter, Harvard Business School Press, 1996

- For a reasonably thorough review of different definitions and explanations of change management try:

  Making Sense of Change Management, Esther Cameron and Mike Green, Kogan Page, 2004

- Six Sigma is a powerful methodology for change and continuous improvement. It is strong in terms of objective setting and being data driven. There are many good books available on this topic. But to get value requires an in-depth understanding of the method, which usually needs more experience and training than a book can provide. However, start with the basics. Some options for straightforward introductory texts are:

  What is Six Sigma?, Pete Pande and Larry Holpp, McGraw-Hill, 2001

  What is Lean Six Sigma?, Mike George, Dave Rowlands and Bill Kastle; McGraw-Hill, 2003

- I frequently make reference to brainstorming. For a good, readable book providing practical approaches to managing creativity with alternative techniques I recommend:

  Non-stop Creativity and Innovation: How to Generate and Implement Winning Ideas, Fiona McLeod and Richard Thomson, McGraw-Hill, 2003

- To understand systems dynamics and the concept of leverage (amongst other things), try:

  The Fifth Discipline: The Art & Practice of the Learning Organization, Peter M. Senge, Random House Business Books, 2006

- There are many books on building teams for projects and change. Creating the right team is an art as well as a science, requiring empathy and an understanding of which people will work well together. Some useful background reading on teams is:

  Team Roles at Work, R. Meredith Belbin, Butterworth–Heinemann, 2003

  Management Teams: Why They Succeed or Fail, R. Meredith Belbin, Butterworth–Heinemann, 2003

- A project manager will bring useful tools, such as risk and issue management, and a good understanding of planning and contingency to any project. If you are not a project manager and you want to get a better understanding of how to create and manage a plan, you can try my sister book to this volume:

  Project Management Step by Step: How to plan and manage a highly successful project, Richard Newton, Prentice Hall, 2006